WHA
GOD
REALLY
WANT?

Beyond the Lies:
How to Overcome Stress &
Live the Promised Abundant Life

Michael Trillo

breakthrough
PUBLISHING

Michael Trillo
6513 132nd Ave NE, Suite #218
Kirkland, WA 98033

ISBN 0-9801288-0-3

978-0-9801288-0-2

Published in Kirkland, Washington by Breakthrough Publishing

www.WhatDoesGodReallyWant.com

www.MichaelTrillo.com

Italics in Scripture quotations are the author's emphasis.

Unless otherwise indicated, Scripture quotations are from:

The Holy Bible, New International Version (NIV)
© 1973, 1984 by International Bible Society, used by permission of Zondervan Publishing House

Other Scripture quotations are from:

New American Standard Bible® (NASB) © 1960, 1977, 1995 by the Lockman Foundation. Used by permission.

This book is not intended to provide medical advice or to take the place of medical advice from and/or treatment by your personal physician. Readers are advised to consult their own doctors or other qualified health professionals regarding the treatment of their medical problems. Neither the publisher nor the author takes any responsibility for any possible consequences resulting from any treatment, actions, or application of medicine, supplement, herb, or preparation used by any person reading or following the information in this book. If any readers are using prescription medications, they should not discontinue those medications to start supplementation without the advice of and proper supervision of a physician.

In order to protect the privacy of certain individuals, stories recorded in this book have been modified. All other stories have been used by permission.

Printed in the United States of America

CONTENTS

PART ONE

How to Identify Counterfeits and Discover Your Purpose

CHAPTER I

STRESS IS AN EPIDEMIC

Even in the Christian World

*Stress is like an iceberg. We can see one-eighth of it above,
but what about what's below?*
—ANONYMOUS

*There is an epidemic in cities everywhere
and the epidemic is stress.*
—ANNE M. VIDOVICH, M.A.

I'm so frustrated with being tired and stressed...
How many times have you had that thought? Regardless of how much you resist it, it keeps swimming through your mind: "I'm stressed and tired, and I don't know why."

Other people appear comfortable in their lifestyles, yet you're plagued with anxiety and exhaustion. Everyone else seems to have the missing piece to life's puzzle...while you don't even have the first clue on how to open the puzzle box.

Ever wondered how much money you've spent in attempting to eliminate stress from your life? You can't wait for the next vacation, the next weekend away, the next relationship, the next big thing...but they all are only temporary escapes from the inevitable. Your search for meaning and relief leaves you empty-handed and several dollars short.

These spiraling frustrations continue to eat away at your energy, leaving you with a hollow feeling inside.

THE STRESS EPIDEMIC

Unfortunately, statistics show that stress has become a way of life for the majority in our society, and much of it occurs in the workplace:

- In a 2001 Gallup poll, U.S. corporations showed that sixty percent of managers felt that stress-related illness was prevalent among their employees. The resulting productivity loss amounted annually to approximately sixteen days of sick leave and $8,000 per person.
- The World Health Organization has declared that job stress has now become a "worldwide epidemic."
- Some estimates show that eighty percent of all visits to physicians are for stress-related disorders.
- According to the National Institute for Occupational Safety and Health, depression—which is one result of stress—is predicted to be the leading occupational disease of the twenty-first century, responsible for more days lost than any other factor.

CHRISTIANS ARE NO DIFFERENT

It's interesting to note that Christians, who profess to follow a supernatural and historical God-man in Jesus Christ, are not an exception to these findings. They are just as stressed and tired as the rest of the world.

Doesn't that seem strange?

Unfortunately, it's true. When it comes to how much stress they experience, many Christians appear to be not much different than the atheist who lives down the street. Could it be that many of us are unknowingly living out Satan's counterfeit life purposes—purposes that look and sound just like the real thing? Could that be the reason for the statistics mentioned above?

After all, Jesus said that those who believe in Him would do the same incredible things He did—and "even greater things" (John 14:12). *Greater* things! If this is true, why have so many Christians become statistics?

Today, we in the Church are suffering from stress just like the rest of the world because of the lies we have unknowingly believed.

PURPOSE AND STRESS

Do you ever stop and try to analyze why you get stressed? Contrary to what you may have always believed, the stress you feel may have nothing at all to do with your circumstances or anything outside of you.

Two people could be experiencing the exact same situation or circumstances. One will end up anxious, and the other will experience continued and consistent excitement about life. What's the difference? The difference is their purpose!

Your purpose will always determine your stress level.

This book will expose the hidden connection between stress and lies, prove that counterfeit life purposes produce stress, and that God's ultimate purpose produces the promised abundant life.

Your purpose will always determine your stress level.

If you could live life filled—not with stress—but with purpose and power, it would be the kind of life reflected in these passages:

The lions may grow weak and hungry, but those who seek the LORD lack no good thing. (Psalm 34:10)

Even youths grow tired and weary, and young men stumble and fall; but those who hope in the LORD will renew their strength. They will soar on wings like eagles; they will run and not grow weary, they will walk and not be faint. (Isaiah 40:30- 31)

I came that they may have life, and have it abundantly. (Jesus, in John 10:10)

We are more than conquerors through him who loved us. (Romans 8:37)

Are you ready to be stronger than a lion? Do you want to "soar on wings like eagles?" How does living life "abundantly" sound to you?

You were born for those "greater things" Jesus spoke of in John 14:12. You were born to walk on water—and deep down you know it! Later on in this book, you'll learn something that's greater than walking on water. You'll see that anyone who really wants to can live a supernatural life.

We've all wondered if there's more to life than the way we're living now. We've wondered, in the back of our minds, if there's more to this "Christianity thing" than what we've seen and experienced.

I'm here to tell you there is.

You may be ready to jump in and say, "Hey, I'd like to live the way Jesus said I could!" But how in the world can I actually do greater things than Jesus Himself did? The necessary first step is to discover and unload the lies you've embraced.

In the Bible there are many accounts of people living this way. I've read other accounts of people today who have done greater things than Christ's disciples. I personally know some of these people. When my wife, Kristy and I started walking toward this way of living, we were absolutely amazed at what we'd been missing.

I believe we all can live this way by living according to our ultimate purpose, based on what the Bible says. I used to be a statistic, living the same kind of stressful life so many others live. I desperately sought the Lord, and gradually the Holy Spirit opened my eyes and showed me the counterfeit purposes I lived by and the lies behind them.

I write this book not as an expert or life guide, but as one who has only begun to discover the powerful truths of the Bible. My life is nowhere close to perfect, even though I have personally gone from struggling with exhaustion, sickness, anxiety and irritability, to living with purpose, joy, peace, strength and good health. More than anything else in life, I desire to know God.

YOUR MOST IMPORTANT PURSUIT

Do you realize that discovering God's purpose for your life is the single most important pursuit you'll ever undertake? As mentioned above, your purpose will always determine your stress level. Living according to your true purpose is the ticket to liberate you from the bondage of stress. Therefore I encourage you to read this book with...

- the Holy Spirit as your Teacher, knowing that your own intellect is limited. Ask Him to give you supernatural wisdom and understanding, opening the eyes of your heart and mind. "He [the Holy Spirit] will guide you into all truth" (John 16:13). Ask Him to help you hear from Him only.
- an open mind. "Instruct a wise man and he will be wiser still" (Proverbs 9:9). If you are humble and starving for God, everyone is your potential teacher in some manner. In contrast, if you think you "know it all" you won't seek to know God better. You will only look for mistakes, inaccuracies, and things to criticize.

I also encourage you to read one chapter a day. This will help you personalize what you read and also give you time to talk about the chapter with your heavenly Father and friends. You should expect to take between twenty to thirty minutes to read each chapter.

If you're the type of reader who likes to pick and choose chapters to read, you might have trouble understanding this book. A logical and biblical foundation has been built as it goes from chapter to chapter. Skipping a chapter may cause you to miss the building blocks needed to fully comprehend what is said.

CLARIFYING THE TERMS

Misunderstanding can sometimes get in the way of capturing the heart of a message. So, for the purpose of clarity, I would like to define the terms I will be using throughout this book:

- *Purpose*—What something is used for; the reason and intention for everything you do. Synonyms: goal, intention, point, objective.
- *Means*—A course of action by which an end or purpose can be achieved. The means to the end (or in this case, the means to fulfilling your purpose) can be accomplished through many different methods. Synonyms: ways, methods.

5

- *Mission*—An assignment one is sent to carry out. One's duty, job description, or responsibility to accomplish an overall purpose or objective. Synonyms: assignment, commission, duty, job description.
- *Results*—A consequence or by-product; outcome or effect. Synonyms: aftermath, fruit, repercussion.

In the next chapter, you will learn the obvious but little known connection between your purpose and stress, and how it affects your life.

SUMMARY

1. Stress has become a worldwide epidemic.
2. Christians tend to be just as stressed as the rest of the world.
3. You were designed to do "greater things," live the abundant life, and soar on wings like eagles.

DISCUSSION QUESTIONS

1. Do you ever struggle with stress?
2. How have you responded to the stress in your life?
3. Have you ever wondered if there was more to the Christian life than what you've experienced?

PRAYER

Lord, please help me listen to Your Holy Spirit.
Open my heart and mind, and give me the wisdom to discover my true
purpose. Release me from any unrealized bondage.
Give me a passion to focus on knowing and loving You more.
I humble myself before You and look forward to learning from Your Spirit.
Thank You, Lord.

CHAPTER 2

STRESS AND PURPOSE

The History and Link between Stress and Your Purpose

*They say that there are two important days in your life: the day
you were born, and the day you find out why you were born.*
—CARL TOWNSEND

*There is no neutral ground in the universe;
every square inch, every split second, is claimed by
God and counter-claimed by Satan.*
—C. S. LEWIS

Everything has a purpose.

Imagine walking into your local hardware store and excitedly making a beeline for the tool section. They've got a new power drill you're planning to buy.

On your way to the drill aisle, you see a new high-tech gadget, like something from the future. It looks cool and complicated—lots of levers, buttons and dials. But what's it for? You stop and spend a few minutes looking at it, trying to guess. You're completely bewildered. Seeing no instruction manual, you ask a passing customer service person what this gadget is.

He hesitates for a second, and then confidently responds, "It's a plunger!"

"Are you serious? But what are all these levers and buttons for?"

He hesitates again. "Oh, it doesn't matter. It would work as a plunger."

You're confused and slightly annoyed. You dismiss him with a polite, "Thanks." But you're way too curious to just let this go. Another customer service person passes by, and you ask the same question: "Excuse me, what is this tool supposed to do?"

She responds without hesitation, "Oh, it can do whatever you want it to. It looks like one of those multi-use tools!"

You realize that you're hearing only worthless opinions and since there doesn't appear to be a way to discover the tool's intended purpose, you continue on your way. That new gizmo—as cool and expensive as it may be, is not worth a penny if you don't know what it's meant to do.

WHAT'S IT FOR?

What did the inventor have in mind when he created that tool? What was his purpose? He obviously designed and built it with a distinct purpose that would benefit others. But if he failed to provide instructions, allowing its intended purpose to remain secret, it's useless.

Even the simplest of tools comes with instructions for use as well as warnings against misuse. If simple tools have purposes and warnings, doesn't it make even more sense that the really important things do too?

Like life?

Just like a tool, when your life is misused, even though your intentions are good, it will function poorly and eventually break down. And the sad thing about life is that the results of your *misuse of life* show up much later, when it can be difficult to change course. That's why it's critical to live according to God's purpose and heed the warnings written in His book, the Bible.

What is your purpose in life? Why did God create you? Are there any areas where you might be unknowingly operating on the basis of lies?

All these questions lead to *the* question: *What does God really want?*

YOUR CORE MOTIVATION

Whether you realize it or not, you're living for something on a daily basis.

Purpose is what drives you to do what you do. Purpose inspires you to jump out of bed every morning. Purpose is your energizer—the gasoline that fuels your emotional engine. Purpose is what empowers you to courageously plow through insurmountable obstacles. Purpose is what brings color to a black and white planet. When you begin to speak and act out of purpose, something extraordinary happens. You live with ease and energy. You're centered and rested, even through the inevitable storms of life.

Without purpose, life is aimless. Empty. It's like being in a boat drifting on the ocean without a compass, or like wandering in a desert without a destination.

Without a purpose, you're not living. You merely exist. You were meant to live the abundant life, not to simply survive. Ants survive. Jesus-followers were meant to live supernaturally.

What if you could wake up each day, knowing that out of a million different purposes you could be living for, you're doing exactly what you were created to do? What if you could tighten up that purpose, certain that everything you study, work on and think about revolves around that one purpose?

> **Make your work to be in keeping with your purpose.**
> **—Leonardo da Vinci**

The Tragedy of Mistaken Purposes

Your purpose will always determine your stress level.

Worse than living without purpose is living out a mistaken purpose based on a lie. It results in stress, exhaustion, busyness, anger, anxiety and depression.

Imagine playing basketball in the NBA Finals, only to make the mistake of shooting at your opponent's goal, yet arguing with the coach and referee that you're shooting at your own goal. Is that not a monumental tragedy?

Most of us have the sense to plan more carefully than that, especially if there's a large investment at stake. But when it comes to the single most important investment we could possibly make, why do we miss the target?

The scariest thing is that many of these mistaken purposes have the appearance of being the right ones. What a sneaky little devil he is! This book exposes the counterfeit purposes authored by the great deceiver to give you awareness of his strategies and sneaky philosophies. "Have nothing to do with the fruitless deeds of darkness, but rather expose them" (Ephesians 5:11).

PURSUIT OF MY PURPOSE

When I was twenty years old, I set out to discover exactly why God had created mankind. I was searching for a foundational purpose that I could hold onto. Surprisingly, I spent the majority of my time discovering what my purpose is not. I found many Bible passages that warn of counterfeit and mistaken purposes and the destructive consequences of living according to them.

I came up with my purpose statement, though I didn't truly understand how to start living out that statement until much later. Until that point, I was unknowingly living out counterfeit purposes, resulting in a life of stress. Sadly, I've personally experienced the bondage and destructive consequences that come with a life that was never intended to be.

THE ORIGIN OF STRESS

While Adam and Eve walked in the lush Garden of Eden, getting their summer tan, they came across a smooth-talking, lying snake, who sold them the lie that they could not trust God. After falling for the lie, they realized they were naked in every way. For the very first time, they felt shame and the need to cover their nakedness.

As they attempted to hide themselves, God called out, asking where they were. Adam gave an interesting answer: "I was afraid because I was naked; so I hid" (Genesis 3:10).

Somehow this simple chain of events had caused Adam to be unreasonably afraid of God. The sad thing is, before that time, he and Eve shared a love relationship with God that was most likely deeper than any humans living on earth have had with Him since. God had done nothing to cause this fear. So why was Adam so afraid?

Let's examine the tragic scenario that occurred in the Garden of Eden:

> Now the serpent was more crafty than any of the wild animals
> the LORD God had made. He said to the woman, "Did God re-
> ally say, 'You must not eat from any tree in the garden?'"

The woman said to the serpent, "We may eat fruit from the trees in the garden, but God did say, 'You must not eat fruit from the tree that is in the middle of the garden, and you must not touch it, or you will die.'"

"You will not surely die," the serpent said to the woman. "For God knows that when you eat of it your eyes will be opened, and you will be like God, knowing good and evil."

When the woman saw that the fruit of the tree was good for food and pleasing to the eye, and also desirable for gaining wisdom, she took some and ate it. She also gave some to her husband, who was with her, and he ate it. Then the eyes of both of them were opened, and they realized they were naked; so they sewed fig leaves together and made coverings for themselves.

Then the man and his wife heard the sound of the LORD God as he was walking in the garden in the cool of the day, and they hid from the LORD God among the trees of the garden. But the LORD God called to the man, "Where are you?"

He answered, "I heard you in the garden, and I was afraid because I was naked; so I hid." (Genesis 3:1- 10)

1. The Original Source: Lies from the snake—"You will not surely die," the serpent said to the women. "For God knows that when you eat of it your eyes will be opened, and you will be like God, knowing good and evil" (Genesis 3:4). Because the snake's intention was to make God look really bad, he questioned two things about God:

First, God's intention toward them: *Does He really mean well?*

Second, the meaning of God's words: *Is that really what He meant?*

Ever since, Satan has been manipulating human relationships in the same way. And the above questions arise not only in relation to God, but also with each other. Ever since then, misunderstanding has been at the root of family conflicts.

I would like to remind you that even though Satan deceives many today, he and each of his crewmembers are on a short leash with God (Luke

10:18-19, Ephesians 1:18-23, Colossians 2:10). We are not to get caught up with fear towards this being. He is a defeated being.

2. The Result: Fear in their hearts—"I was afraid because I was naked; so I hid" (Genesis 3:10). Fear has been the shadow and echo of every lie ever since. Lies always result in fear: Will God really provide for me? Will God really protect me? Does He really approve of me?

3. Their Strategy: To hide behind fig leaves—"Then the eyes of both of them were opened, and they realized they were naked; so they sewed fig leaves together and made coverings for themselves" (Genesis 3:7). Since then, society's main strategy is to hide imperfections and hurts through socially acceptable means—a fabricated personality.

4. The Long-Term Effect—Disconnection and separation from God, others, and self.

THE RESULT OF THE LIE

One of the best strategies for winning a battle is to know your enemy's plan of attack. Since the episode in the Garden of Eden, Satan's plan has been the same:

1. His Purpose—Your separation from God, others and yourself (See Genesis 3:1-10).

2. His Strategy—Sneaky lies, creative counterfeits. "When he lies, he speaks his native language, for he is a liar and the father of lies" (John 8:44).

3. His Method—Attacking and accusing the intentions and motives of others, twisting words to create misunderstanding. "For the accuser of our brothers, who accuses them before our God day and night, has been hurled down" (Revelation 12:10).

When you follow the trail of relational conflicts, lies are usually found at the root. When you misunderstand another person's words or motives, unforgiveness and bitterness often result. Lies cause separation from God, others and from self. From the separation you suffer these two results: Fear and bitterness.

1. Fear and anxiety about God's love—Satan wants you to question whether God really loves you enough to protect and provide for you. He wants you to question whether God really cares and delights in you unconditionally.

2. Bitterness and anger toward others and self—Satan wants you to accuse others' intentions and project on them your own presumptions. He wants you to misunderstand other people's words and to become defensive, putting up walls against others. He wants you to condemn yourself for all of your mistakes and failures.

Satan is the father of all lies, the author of deceit. He's the mentor behind every liar, cheater and thief. Did you know that many of his lies are biblically based, with a clever and delicate twist? And they always come with a price.

Lies produce fear and bitterness.

The more you think about Satan's lies, the greater your fear becomes. Fear has many culturally acceptable faces and names: stress, anxiety, pressure, concern, worry, nervousness. In our society today, many common fears exist. These fears have a way of sneaking into many of your daily activities and your interaction with others. The five most common include:

- Fear of failure
- Fear of rejection
- Fear of pain and death
- Fear of poverty
- Fear of abandonment

Fear is the anticipation of pain. It typically starts with two words: *What if?* The trigger to fear-based thinking is imagining an undesirable event that will, in reality, most likely never occur.

Mark Twain put it this way: "I have lived a long life and had many troubles, most of which never happened." For the most part, what you fear is an illusion—a mirage. It's most often based on lies. I once heard Zig Ziglar explain fear with this acronym: False Evidence Appearing Real.

Fear will forever live imprisoned in a future that will most likely never happen. If you live in anxiety you are imprisoned by your own imagination, and because of this, you miss out on the enjoyment of the present.

Our society labels all these emotions under a single word—*Stress.*

Living with fear and bitterness always results in stress. This does not mean that all stress is a direct result of fear and bitterness. Stress most certainly can have other causes such as combat trauma, death of a loved one, rape, etc.

THERE'S HOPE: GOD'S IMPLANTED BEACON SIGNAL

Fortunately, God provided you a "beacon signal," a method of bringing you back home to Himself when you wander away listening to lies. What a great God we serve!

When a U.S. fighter plane gets shot down while flying above enemy territory, the pilot's last resort for survival is to physically eject from the plane. Imagine the frightening trek ahead of him—to make his way through the jungles or the desert inside enemy territory, constantly wondering if his next step will be his last.

In the past, pulling that eject lever was nearly always a choice between getting blown up in the skies or dying at the hands of the enemy. That is, until 1982.

In that year, the military invented a clever way to save these fallen warriors. Personal Locator Beacons (PLB's) are techno gadgets that send out encrypted radio signals, allowing these freedom fighters to be located by a satellite system. A search and rescue team is then sent to locate them.

God hardwired you with an internal beacon signal. This divinely planted beacon signal is the desperate voice inside of you crying out to be loved and valued. You were designed in such a way that you would long for your Maker—so He could bring you back to Himself. It's an internal signal that says, "I am in urgent need of God!"

Regardless of how often you may deny your built-in hunger for love, this internal hunger is always crying out to be fed, frantically consuming any iota of love that comes your way. You might as well have a sticky note on your forehead that says, "Please love me!"

Every human being who has ever lived has experienced this unquenchable thirst buried deep inside that only God can satisfy. When your satisfaction is not found in God, the consequences appear in your emotions. You're anxious, stressed, angry, disappointed and depressed. Physically, you suffer with exhaustion, sickness, neck and back pain, high blood pressure, insomnia, fatigue and more. Every last atom in your body is craving the approval of the Creator of the universe.

O God, you are my God, earnestly I seek you; my soul thirsts for you, my body longs for you, in a dry and weary land where there is no water. (Psalm 63:1)

My soul yearns, even faints, for the courts of the LORD; my heart and my flesh cry out for the living God. (Psalm 84:2)

THE DEEPEST LONGING OF YOUR HEART

Pain was designed to alert you of danger to your physical health. Stress (fear and bitterness) is to your heart what pain is to your body, a built-in alarm system warning you that a counterfeit purpose has sneaked past your lie detector. It is your heart's way of telling you there's a threat to your life. God designed your body so you would listen to the cries of your heart.

This deep, desperate desire to be loved trumpets itself publicly in ways like these:

- You brag about what you own, who you know, what you know, what you've done and where you've been.
- You exaggerate when telling stories.
- You chase after the business/success trap.
- You buy bigger and better things you don't need, with money you don't have, to impress people who don't care.
- You look at yourself in every mirror to make sure you always look impressive.
- You passionately desire to lose weight in order to be acceptable by society's standards.

- You keep your opinions quietly to yourself for fear of being rejected.
- You find yourself talking more than listening.
- You avoid conflict at all costs, for fear of rejection or abandonment.
- You volunteer your free time at church or for other noble causes, at the expense of time with your family, because you want to feel like your doing something significant.

As a general rule, we attempt to use our original, God-created roles as men and women to fill our need to be significant and to be loved. Men tend to look for this fulfillment in their work. They pride themselves in being competent and intelligent. They often dream about being publicly commended for a "job well done." Women typically try to fill this need through relationships. The woman was designed to be the man's helper, so it's natural for her to want to be loved by a man. Women dream about being romanced by a strong and loving man.

Some of you manage this desire to be loved by stuffing it down or denying it. You masterfully train your mind to never get disappointed or hurt by others. I'm well aware of this because I've done it myself.

You need to realize that severe emotional and physical damage result when you stuff down your emotions and pretend that they don't exist. If you train your mind to deny the gigantic pink elephant in the room—the relentless voice within calling for God's love and approval—you deceive yourself into thinking you don't need love.

WHEN YOU STUFF IT DOWN

In the 1930's, New York Yankees' first baseman Lou Gehrig was called the Iron Horse because he refused to take a day off from work. For over six decades he held the record for the most consecutive games played—2,130.

But medical examination revealed that every one of his fingers had been broken, some more than once. He suffered from ALS (amyotrophic lateral sclerosis), a muscle-wasting disease, which eventually became known as Lou Gehrig's Disease.

In later research of this disease, physician and best-selling author Dr.

Gabor Mate observed common characteristics in those who suffer from it. They're the nicest people you'll ever meet, they never ask for help, they never admit to emotional or physical pain and they never complain. Dr. Mate's findings convinced him that the emotional management style of these patients might have triggered their illness.

In his book, *When the Body Says No: Understanding the Cost of Hidden Stress,* Dr. Gabor Mate uses examples from two decades of medical practice to demonstrate how stuffing down stress helps cause this disease.

Each of you has an urgent yearning to be loved and approved.

You live dangerously when you deny the existence of your heart, and believe the lie that life is all about living in your head. You can't silence this built-in beacon signal any more than you could silence an alarm system using a pillow.

GOD'S LOVE AND APPROVAL

Since God, your divine architect, designed you with this hunger for His love and approval, you live your life either motivated by His love and approval, or in a desperate attempt to win His love and approval.

If you live *from* God's love and approval, you trust in what He tells you through His Word, and you have experienced His forgiveness, acceptance and unconditional love. You know and believe that God is happy with you because you belong to Him. You don't believe God condemns you or is angry with you any longer for all your mistakes.

If you live *for* God's love and approval, you're attempting the most unattainable feat known to mankind. You know about God's love, but either have not received it or have not really believed that He loves you unconditionally. You have stuffed down your need for love, and you look for that love in all the wrong places. Your dying words are: "I know God loves me. I just don't feel it."

Every counterfeit purpose is motivated by the need to attain God's approval. You're either extravagantly celebrating your journey back home to your perfect heavenly Dad, or you're desperately searching for Him in all the wrong places.

17

In the next chapter, you'll learn what God truly wants, as well as four of the most common counterfeit purposes and lies of Satan that Christians fall for when they are trying to earn God's love and approval.

SUMMARY

1. God created you with a definite purpose in mind.
2. Satan twisted God's truth and created compelling counterfeit purposes.
3. The result of the lies: stress from fear and bitterness.
4. God's beacon signal: your desperate need to be loved.
5. You either live *from* or *for* God's love and approval.
6. Counterfeit purposes are motivated by the need to attain God's approval.

DISCUSSION QUESTIONS

1. If someone evaluated your life, what one-sentence statement do you think they would give to describe your purpose?
2. Do you operate your life *from* or *for* God's love and approval?
3. Do you ever stuff down your feelings, dreams, fears and frustrations?

PRAYER

Lord Jesus, please help me to continually humble myself.
Open the eyes of my heart so I can see what I'm really living for.
Show me what You really want.
Help me to break through my fears and live on purpose,
rather than by default.
Thank You in advance for giving me a reason to live!

CHAPTER 3

THE BATTLE OF PURPOSES

God's Purpose vs. Counterfeit Purposes

*Efforts and courage are not enough
without purpose and direction.*
—JOHN F. KENNEDY

*The supreme end of education is expert discernment in
all things—the power to tell the good from the bad,
the genuine from the counterfeit, and to prefer the
good and the genuine to the bad and the counterfeit.*
—UNKNOWN

Every great company writes a statement of its purpose or mission. This purpose statement is a declaration that is intended to drive every objective, goal and plan. Here are the purpose statements from two well-known companies:

Microsoft: To help people and businesses throughout the world realize their full potential.

Nike: To bring inspiration and innovation to every athlete in the world.

Each of these companies exists to fulfill its purpose statement. Employees work together to fulfill that one purpose. Imagine this hypothetical scenario: I gather all the Microsoft workers together in a gigantic auditorium and ask them, "What is Bill Gates' purpose for this company?" They would probably shout simultaneously, "Bill wants us to help people and businesses throughout the world realize their full potential."

Then I randomly point to Sally, one of the Microsoft workers, and ask her to describe her job. She might say, "I'm a software developer," or "I'm a supervisor." Her job description or personal mission helps to accomplish the overall purpose of the company.

If you were to ask God to write a purpose statement for your life, what do you think He would write?

LIFE'S PURPOSE STATEMENT, ACCORDING TO JESUS

One of the Pharisees, who happened to be a guru when it came to the law, wanted to test Jesus with this question: "Teacher, which is the greatest commandment in the Law?"

Jesus replied; "'Love the Lord your God with all your heart and with all your soul and with all your mind.' This is the first and greatest commandment. And the second is like it; 'Love your neighbor as yourself.' All the Law and the Prophets hang on these two commandments" (Matthew 22:35- 40).

Jesus is simply saying you are to love God and love others like you love yourself. Don't you just love simplicity? It just makes everything so…simple!

Love happens in the context of relationships. Relationships are never static; they are either developing or deteriorating. Therefore, based on what Jesus said, a concise summary of your purpose statement would be this:

To develop loving relationships with God, others and myself.

Your purpose is to develop loving relationships (Matthew 22:35-40; see also Romans 13:9; Galatians 5:14; James 2:8). Knowledge is a means to that end. The fruit of that end is obedience to God, ministry, character growth and discovering your personal mission.

MEANS	END	RESULT
KNOWLEDGE	**DEVELOP LOVING RELATIONSHIPS**	**FRUITS**
Read & Study Bible Read Christian books Listen to sermons Learn from believers	Intimacy Connectedness Closeness Familiarity	Obedience to God Ministry Character growth Personal Mission

THE SLIPPERY PATH TO PURPOSE

The slope starts to become slippery when you focus on gaining knowledge, or producing fruit, as more important than your relationship with God. These slippery paths are rooted in Satan's counterfeit purposes, motivated by the lie that you have to perform to gain God's approval.

When you live out God's purpose, you experience a variety of results.

- Worshiping and glorifying God are fruits that result from learning how loving He is.
- Becoming like Christ is the fruit of spending time with Him, just as you tend to adopt the traits of a friend you spend time with.
- Sharing with others about God's love is merely a means of bragging about Who you know.
- You follow His rules because you love Him and want to obey Him.
- Serving Him fully in ministry is an overflow of your heart that has been transformed by love.
- Wise stewardship and management of financial resources is the fruit that results from understanding His loving provision.
- You make the decision to stay pure when you see the beauty of His holiness.

FRUITFULNESS

When was the last time you saw a fruit tree grunting in an effort to produce fruit? Can you imagine such a scene? If you simply water the root of a fruit tree, it will effortlessly bear fruit. You'll never see that tree grunting or shaking. If you do, you should immediately consult a psychiatrist. Watering the root is the deepening of your relationship with God.

The Lord Jesus invites you to remain in Him:

Remain in me, and I will remain in you. No branch can bear
fruit by itself; it must remain in the vine. Neither can you bear

fruit unless you remain in me. I am the vine; you are the branches. If a man remains in me and I in him, he will bear much fruit; apart from me you can do nothing. (John 15:4-5)

As a natural consequence of remaining in Him and staying close to Him, you'll bear much fruit. If you want to change the fruit you're producing, you must first change the root purpose of your life. Otherwise, producing fruit in the flesh is only a tiring way to live.

EFFORTLESS

One mid-summer day in Atlanta, I was sitting across from my friend Chris outside Starbucks. I was sharing with him from the principles God had shown me—that life is not about simply pursuing knowledge or doing good works only; rather, you should use knowledge to pursue a deep friendship with God that will result in good works.

If you want to change the fruit you're producing, you must first change the root purpose of your life.

Chris looked at me as if he'd never heard this concept before. I encouraged him to spend the first hour of his day worshipping, sharing and listening to the Lord.

A week later, Chris called, and His first words were, "Effortless, Mike. Effortless!" Suddenly, sharing the gospel, loving others and staying pure were absolutely effortless for him! He said he never knew life could be so easy!

THE LIE-DRIVEN PURPOSE: TO EARN GOD'S LOVE

Everybody has an inborn need to be approved and loved. We all have the tendency to believe the lie that we need to earn as well as maintain God's love and approval. We then begin making plans that we think will help us to achieve this unattainable goal.

We typically believe this lie as a result of how we were parented, or because of situations we've observed in our past. Let's look at four of the most common counterfeit purposes we use to earn God's love, illustrated by four fictional individuals.

1. KEN KNOWLEDGE

Ken unknowingly believes a lie that knowledge can win him the approval of God and men. He has very strong analytical and problem-solving skills. He appears to implicitly trust his own intellect and logical thinking. He doesn't talk much about his personal friendship with God.

In reality, Ken has never learned how to deal with emotional pain. He stuffs things that are too painful to deal with. Because he refuses to admit his relational needs and desires, his disappointments reveal themselves in over-reactive tendencies. He has great difficulty allowing others to communicate their feelings. He often corrects them for being too "emotional."

Ken tries to earn God's approval by regularly pursuing new nuggets of "Aha!" information from the Bible. To him, the Bible is a textbook rather than a personal love letter. God is simply a cosmic entity to be studied and scrutinized. Ken is like a professor, devoid of any personal touch or emotion. Ken doesn't see God as a smiling dad, laughing and playing with His kids. When Ken teaches at church, his message is an academic experience void of any relational dynamics.

Ken lives in a theoretical reality and often judges others for not studying enough. He doesn't see people as those he can know, love, or enjoy. Rather, he sees them as students to be educated. From Ken's point of view, it's more important to be accurate than to be an understanding friend.

Marriage Comparison

When Ken and Kelly first got married, Ken asked her to make an instructional video explaining what would make her happy in their relationship. It was jam-packed, relaying her deepest desires and needs. Unfortunately, Ken spent most of his time watching the video, using a dictionary to define every word and dissecting every phrase.

Meanwhile Kelly waited and watched, longing for him to turn off the video and spend some personal time with her. One day, Ken came home and flopped a dozen red roses on the kitchen counter without a single word to her. He then turned and headed to the living room to study the video. Hesitant, Kelly blurted, "They're beautiful. Except, you just don't do that without saying anything."

Ken responded, "Well, what do you want me to say?"

Kelly frowned. "I can't tell you what to say. It's supposed to come from your heart."

Upon hearing this, Ken's brain malfunctioned and suffered a seizure. He had no idea how to process what it meant for something to "come from your heart."

Proper Perspective

It may be difficult for some of you to believe that there are actually people who act like Ken did towards his wife. But many people act the same way toward God. Absurd as it may seem, most Christians have followed this path at one time or another.

> *Three of the most dangerous words in the English language are: I know that.*

Three of the most dangerous words in the English language are: *I know that.* This mindset becomes a lethal cancer that slowly kills relationships. For many people, knowledge has become a handicap. "Knowledge puffs up, but love builds up" (1 Corinthians 8:1).

As we discussed earlier, knowledge is a *necessary* means to the end, not an end in itself. When Jesus lived on earth, He sharply rebuked the religious people of the day for nitpicking others with their knowledge of the law, but not knowing the God Who wrote the law.

> "You diligently study the Scriptures because you think that by them you possess eternal life. These are the Scriptures that testify about me, yet you refuse to come to me to have life." (John 5:39-40)

As a result of Ken's inability to manage his emotional pain, he resorted to stuffing his emotions. This was partly the result of believing a message our society tends to project, that real men are not emotional. Sadly, the feelings he so vehemently denies eventually morph into fear and bitterness, manifesting themselves in defensiveness and disconnectedness.

Imagine what it would be like if you continually stuffed garbage under your living room carpet. After a few weeks, there would be a mound so huge and smelly that you couldn't have a conversation over it. In the same way, unless Ken learns how to share his stuffed emotions with God, he'll never see how his emotional mound is affecting all of his social interactions.

Trust in him at all times, O people; pour out your hearts to him, for God is our refuge. (Psalm 62:8)

Cast all your anxiety on him because he cares for you. (1 Peter 5:7)

My Personal Experience

For a long time, I struggled with this kind of imbalance. I feel that I can describe Ken's innermost feelings because I believed the same lies he does.

When I learned how to receive God's love, my life was suddenly and profoundly changed beyond my wildest dreams. Now, rather than seeing the Bible as a mere textbook, the Bible has become a beautiful and powerful means to an end. I read, not out of attempting to gain God's approval, but out of the presumption that I'm already loved and approved of.

I found that as I got to know God in a deeper, more intimate way, I became more and more immersed in true worship. He opens the eyes of my heart and connects with me in a very personal way when we spend time together.

My marriage is the next area that has benefited by a transformed belief system. In the past, we had read countless marriage books, and although they offered help, we still had a sense that there was more. When we came to truly receive God's love and acceptance, our marriage took a gigantic leap forward.

2. PAULA PERFECTIONIST

Paula unknowingly believes the lie that unless she's perfect, neither God nor people will approve of her. Paula believes in performance-based approval. Paula is always too busy and typically lives in a frantic panic mode. Her to-do list is a mile long.

She sees God as a good Father who's disappointed with her imperfections. However much she tries, it's just never enough. From her viewpoint, the Bible is the perfect recipe for perfection. This is why, after a tiring day at work, she chooses not to read the Bible. It's too tiring to read, since she reads it through a how-to-be-perfect mindset.

Paula views people as objects to be fixed, not as people to know, enjoy and empower. She often struggles with internal anger toward others, though she never expresses this outwardly.

As a mother, Paula has a tendency to correct her children for making a "mess" around the house. For her, it's more important that the house is perfect than it is to teach her children wisdom and responsibility. Her children have learned "mess prevention," rather than to be responsible.

It's often difficult to encourage Paula since she doesn't receive encouragement graciously. She seems to find ways to either deflect praise or to find something else that needs work. She does the same thing with others. When you say something good about a person, Paula is likely to say something like, "True, even though she's a little careless with her money, bless her heart."

As a result of being so hard on herself all her life, she views confrontation as more rejection. When you confront her, you're destroying her idol of perfection.

Marriage Comparison

Paula comes home exhausted from a twelve-hour workday and immediately jumps into cleaning the kitchen, doing the laundry, cooking dinner and paying the bills. Not only is she dead tired, she has been scolding herself all day because just before she had left for work, she accidentally broke one of her husband's tools.

When Patrick, her husband, gets home, he notices the broken tool in the garage and casually asks Paula what happened to the tool. She snaps back, "It's not like I meant to break it! I work so hard all day, and then I slave away doing everything here at home, so please get off my back about your tool!" She has magnified her failure to the point of self-hatred. The sad thing is that Patrick had planned to reassure her that it was no big deal. But since Paula won't talk to him, she is now focused on punishing herself during her self-imposed pity party.

A single lie in Paula's thinking—rejection due to imperfection—caused this tragic scenario. The inevitable result is division within their marriage.

Proper Perspective

Satan is the "accuser" (Revelation 12:10, Zechariah 3:1).

He points at you with his bony finger, focusing on all your failures. His goal is to accuse you and create copies of himself—mini-faultfinders, little accusers of the brothers. Don't get me wrong. Corrections have their proper and necessary place in relationships. But in this instance I'm discussing priorities and focus. When your conversation is only about mistakes and failures, you may be living like Satan's disciple, all for the sake of being "good."

Perfectionism is not a legitimate personality trait.

Sinners could hang out with Jesus, and somehow He didn't turn them off, even with all their imperfections. Instead, He magnetically attracted them to Himself. The only people Jesus consistently rebuked were the religious leaders of the day.

As much as you might believe otherwise, perfectionism is not a legitimate personality trait. Too many people have used the excuse that perfectionism caused this or that, when in reality it is a lethal and poisonous lie that slowly kills. Perfectionism makes you stressed, discontent, tired, critical, crabby and resistant to correction.

The Bible is explicit in what it says about this enslaving lie:

Are you so foolish? After beginning with the Spirit, are you now trying to attain your goal by human effort?... All who rely on

27

observing the law are under a curse.... It is for freedom that Christ has set us free. Stand firm, then, and do not let yourselves be burdened again by a yoke of slavery.... You who are trying to be justified by law have been alienated from Christ. (Galatians 3:3,10; 5:1,4)

This yoke of slavery targets the mind, playing into the way the human mind works. What would happen if someone told you, "Don't think about pink elephants, don't think about pink elephants!" You guessed it. You'd have large pink elephants dancing in your mind for awhile. This is a proven principle about the human mind: *What you think about expands.*

This principle applies to the practice of what I call "sin-sniffing." When you go hunting for failure, you'll find it in everyone, including yourself. Self-condemnation will become your shadow.

My Personal Experience

Over time, God has been healing me from the curse of perfectionism. In the past, I've struggled to grasp the truth that God accepts me with no strings attached. In my struggle, I had bought into the cultural lie that character growth and personal development are ends in themselves.

Whenever I met someone, I would tend to pinpoint faults and weaknesses, just the way Satan does. I meant well, guiding others toward perfection, as I promoted good behavior and discouraged bad behavior. But now that the Lord has changed my heart, I want more than anything to help others experience the beautiful intimacy available with their heavenly Dad.

God has never shown me a list of all my failures. "If you, O Lord, kept a record of sins, O Lord, who could stand? But with you there is forgiveness; therefore you are feared" (Psalm 130:3- 4). If He did keep a record, it would take an immense hard drive to contain all my failures, and just the knowledge that He was keeping track would break me. To my endless relief, He has shown me that He greatly delights in me, in spite of my imperfections and faults.

3. HARRY HAPPY-CHASER

To Harry, feeling happy is an eternal pursuit—an end in itself. This is Harry's way of medicating his unfulfilled longing for love. He seems to think that it is God's responsibility to make him feel good at all times. He often pursues the emotional highs that come from spiritual events—camps, seminars and mission trips. He's more excited about the great things God is doing than he is about God Himself.

As he reads the Bible, he's often looking for a feel good experience. When that doesn't happen, he blames God. He's always looking for the next big thing. The media, always pushing for the next big upcoming attraction, has popularized this type of mindset.

Harry is typically the life of the party, the one everyone calls when there's a get-together. They view him as someone who loves to laugh, someone who's fired up for the Lord and always in the center of ministry; although he also is viewed as moody.

Marriage Comparison

Harry struggles with all the work involved in being married to Henrietta. While they were dating, he had enjoyed the flirting and fun, but that seemed effortless compared to being married. Harry doesn't know it, but he swallowed the lie that it's his wife's job to make him happy. He had believed that marriage would be mostly fun and little work, that the honeymoon would never end.

Today at the office he experienced a tough situation with a disrespectful employee. Instead of facing his anger and processing his frustration, he took his anger home. After describing his rotten day to Henrietta he got upset when she responded, "Well, why didn't you say something to him?" Harry hates it when she confronts him, especially when she's right.

Proper Perspective

Emotions simply reflect the content of your thinking. When Harry's down, he usually follows an unbiblical thought process—stinking thinking. When you dwell on the ways you've failed today, you're always going to feel bad. Emotions are the echoes of your thought processes.

Harry has never been taught to responsibly manage his thoughts. Underneath a depressed emotion is a form of fear and bitterness toward self and others. Harry believes that the benefits associated with knowing God should be his ultimate pursuit. It's all about what he can get from God to make him happy—instead of developing an intimate relationship with his heavenly Dad.

My Personal Experience

I struggled with this problem from my late teens to my mid-twenties. My wife might argue that it went all the way to my late twenties. I thoroughly enjoyed the emotional fruit that God and ministry brought me and unwittingly pursued regular emotional highs. I even measured my friendship with God based on the number of emotional peaks I experienced.

As a result of believing the pursuit of happiness lie, I regularly struggled with bouts of depression and discouragement. I spent a considerable amount of time picturing worst-case scenarios, rooted in my unwise diet of bad news via the television and newspaper.

The Lord has since taught me the power of gratitude and worship as I started the habit of worshiping Him throughout the day. When I managed my thoughts carefully, no longer entertaining the what-ifs that typically danced across my mind, I was much happier and more stable emotionally. "The Lord is my strength and my shield; my heart trusts in him, and I am helped. My heart leaps for joy and I will give thanks to him in song" (Psalm 28:7).

4. MARTHA MINISTRY-MACHINE

Martha believes the lie that God's approval of her is based on how successful she is in ministry. She's secretly addicted to the praise she receives for her good works. In her eyes, to rest and relax is unproductive and a waste of time. She sees God as a workaholic and believes the lie that He's concerned about others in need, but He's not concerned about her personally.

She makes herself sick with an excessive amount of ministry, while neglecting her sleep, nutrition, family and friends. She doesn't believe in a God of rest and meditation. Life is simply too short for that. Martha measures a person's value by how hard she or he works. Constant serving is the only way to "win" God's favor, and serving the Church is the ultimate expression of godliness. She wants people to join her in her frantic lifestyle of serving the body of Christ.

Others see her as hard working, dedicated. They love to be around her, since she radiates energy and purpose, though they're often left wanting for more.

Martha tends to view the Bible as a manual to assist in recruiting and training more busy workers. All her conversations center around ministry—her vision, successes, struggles, goals, numbers and contacts. Sadly, she rarely mentions her personal relationship with God.

Marriage Comparison

When Martha and Mark first got married, Martha committed to serve Mark at all costs. After compiling a list of his needs, she set out to do a thorough and excellent job of washing and ironing his clothes, cooking his meals, cleaning the house, mowing the lawn, fixing things around the house, etc.

Meanwhile, Mark often waited for her to take a break just so he could spend some time with her. One day he asked her to stop working so they could talk and finally catch up with each other. Abruptly she replied, "Listen, honey, I'm just way too busy taking care of you. I don't have time right now." And she rushed off to the garage.

This marriage has suffered over the years from a severe lack of intimacy. Yes, Mark is served well in many areas, and the house is clean and in good repair, but the marriage relationship is slowly dying.

Proper Perspective

Just before Jesus started His ministry, John the Baptist baptized Him. Jesus told John that He needed to be baptized to fulfill what was written. Here's the scene after Jesus was baptized:

As soon as Jesus was baptized, he went up out of the water. At that moment heaven was opened, and he saw the Spirit of God descending like a dove and lighting on him. And a voice from heaven said, "This is my Son, whom I love; with him I am well pleased." (Matthew 3:16- 17)

Jesus hadn't yet started His ministry or done His "work" so why was His Father pleased? Jesus started His ministry *from* His Father's approval—not *for* His Father's approval. For you as well, it makes God happy when you trust and believe what He has said, because true belief always results in loving acts. "The only thing that counts is faith expressing itself through love" (Galatians 5:6). True faith is always validated by love.

Jesus started His ministry from His Father's approval— not for His Father's approval.

The amazing truth is that God would rather be our *Dad* than our *Employer*. When you spend your time with God, it's important not to immediately bring up all your ministry issues. You are not your work. God wants you to get to know Him outside of work and ministry. He desires for you to know Him above all. He desires to disclose His heart and thoughts about *you!* He's much more interested in you as an individual than He is with your work for Him. Your work for Him is merely the byproduct of your intimate relationship with Him.

He desires for you to experience Him deeply, and this will result in bearing *much* fruit in your life. As Jesus said,

"I am the vine; you are the branches. If a man remains in me and I in him, he will bear much fruit; apart from me you can do nothing." (John 15:5)

My Personal Experience

I used to be in full-time ministry as a youth leader. One of the reasons I left is that I got lost in the ministry. I had forgotten exactly why I was doing it. I had lived my life based on my knowledge, skills, gifting and talent. I had forgotten to nurture our love relationship while I served Him.

Since then, I've learned from studying the Old Testament that my friendship with Him is infinitely more important than anything I can do for Him. I'm not inferring that it has to be either-or. I'm saying that my friendship with Him is much more important. Ministry is only the overflow, the outpouring resulting from my time alone with Him.

As we know from studying Scripture, before God sent His servants into service, He often met with them in the desert. It was in the desert of isolation that these warriors drew close to God—Moses, John the Baptist, Paul, the children of Israel and Jesus Himself. It's our choice whether or not we create that desert experience daily—free from distractions, for the sake of being in His presence, and getting to know God in a personal way.

In repentance and rest is your salvation, in quietness and trust is your strength. (Isaiah 30:15)

THE RESULT OF COUNTERFEIT PURPOSES: STRESS

Stress is a direct result of living by Satan's counterfeit purposes.

If you are one who often talks about a stressful day, you're probably someone who's trying to find your way home to God's loving arms through different paths, all paved with lies. To find relief from your stress you start to use "emotional anesthetics" or God replacements: TV, video games, Internet, work, sex, food, etc.

Denied something that it desperately needs, your heart will eventually give birth to addictive emotional anesthetics. Every addiction is rooted in the need to be loved. Every addiction is a form of slavery and idolatry, a replacement for your loving God.

Using emotional anesthetics to manage your emotional needs is like a child covering his face with his hands while playing peek-a-boo, believing he's invisible. It doesn't work. It's about as effective as putting a band-aid on a broken bone.

What are you supposed to do about this gnawing feeling inside, this desperate need to be accepted and approved by God? Why the gigantic gap between knowing about the truth and actually believing it in your heart?

In the next chapter, you will learn what God's ultimate purpose is for your life, and what exactly fills this constant longing you have inside.

SUMMARY

1. Your life purpose is to develop loving relationships with God, others and yourself.
2. Every counterfeit purpose is motivated by a desire for God's love and approval.
3. Counterfeit purposes produce stress.
4. There's a big difference between "knowing about" and "believing in your heart."

DISCUSSION QUESTIONS

1. If you asked your closest friends and family, which of the counterfeit purposes would they say you struggle with?
2. Would they say you're a critical and judgmental person?
3. Do you struggle with just knowing and not truly believing?
4. Do you struggle with stress and anxiety?

PRAYER

Lord, open my eyes by the power of Your Holy Spirit, and show me if I'm living like a Pharisee in any way. I don't want to live like that, for You know how much I want to know and love You. Forgive me for living without believing. I want to love You with all my heart, soul, mind and strength. It's the least I can do in light of all You've done for me. May Your Word and the power of Your Spirit guide me to that end. Thank You, Lord!

CHAPTER 4

WHAT GOD REALLY WANTS

Living Your Purpose Statement

Our greatest joy and our greatest pain
come in our relationships with others.
—STEPHEN R. COVEY

Life is relationships; the rest is just details.
—GARY SMALLEY

Life's Purpose Statement: To develop loving relationships with God, others and yourself.

Jesus boiled everything down to "Love God and love people," teaching us that love is at the heart of all the law and the prophets. In other words, love is at the core of life.

I think I would have had one big problem with Jesus' response if I had been there. I learned long ago that, like everyone else, my natural tendency is to be less than loving. How would I ever live up to this simple but seemingly impossible challenge to love an invisible God, and to love unlovable people, let alone love myself?

Well, thank God He addresses this difficult question in His instruction book, the Bible.

Here's the life-changing concept, the verse that not only blew the lid right off my old mindset, but also absolutely revolutionized my life: "We love because he first loved us" (1 John 4:19).

INDEBTED TO OUR DAD

The fact that Jesus received the death sentence on my behalf answers my issue with this.

The word *indebted* means "owing gratitude or recognition to another for help or favors." Most of us respond naturally to generosity with a sense of indebtedness. The greater the gift or sacrifice, the more we feel we owe something in return. I call this the *Indebtedness Principle.*

You might respond to receiving a valuable gift by saying, "Oh, I can't believe you would do that! How can I ever thank you?" We see this response in Scripture: "How can I repay the LORD for all his goodness to me?" (Psalm 116:12).

Anyone who ever teaches that God's love and grace is a license to sin is someone who has never experienced grace.

Anyone who ever teaches that God's love and grace is a license to sin is someone who has never experienced grace. The *Indebtedness Principle,* rooted in God's unconditional love, is one of the most powerful forces in the universe. This force is so far reaching and widespread that renowned sociologist Alvin Gouldner reported that there is no human society that does not subscribe to this principle.

YOUR DIVINE ATTORNEY

Imagine driving down the street, as you head to a very important job interview.

You're eating a sandwich snugly tucked in its wrapper. Though you try to be careful, you accidentally drop your sandwich and stain your pristine white shirt. You yell profanities. Distracted and fuming over the stain, you suddenly feel a thump—you've hit something! You immediately slam on the brakes and notice a woman screaming at you. Your car has hit her three-year-old son.

Fast forward to nine months later. You've been sentenced to eight years in prison for manslaughter. It's the end of life as you know it. Will you be beaten up, raped, or even killed in prison? What will your friends and family think of you? What kind of job could you get after release? Anguish and grief wash over you like a tidal wave.

Without any warning, your personal attorney, Jesse Christus, who's also been a trusted advisor and a surprisingly good friend through this nightmarish ordeal, requests a private consultation with the judge. Forty-five minutes later, he comes out with a forced smile. "I have great news," he says. "You won't have to serve time in prison. The judge is allowing me to serve your sentence in your place."

You look at him in complete disbelief, wondering if he's lost his mind or if this could be some kind of cruel joke. He reassures you with a letter from the judge, confirming the best news you've ever heard. You tearfully hug him and thank him.

Eight years later, when Jesse is finally released from prison, will you cancel all other plans in order to welcome him back to society? Of course you will! And if Jesse asked to stay at your home for a while, you would be thrilled to have the opportunity to "pay back" this man, if only in a small way, because of the sacrifice he made for you.

You would love him in return because he first loved you.

God initiated the first step toward you by making Himself vulnerable. He did this to show you that He loved you first—undeservingly and sacrificially.

ORPHANS IN NEED OF A PERFECT DAD

Jesus came so we could be reconciled to our heavenly Dad, as Scripture makes clear:

> For if, when we were God's enemies, we were reconciled to Him through the death of His Son, how much more, having been reconciled, shall we be saved through His life! (Romans 5:10)

All this is from God, who reconciled us to Himself through Christ and gave us the ministry of reconciliation. (2 Corinthians 5:18)

After an argument with a friend that makes you decide never to speak again with him, the relationship is broken. Reconciliation is necessary to restore the friendship you once had. To reconcile means to reestablish, settle, or restore a close relationship between people.

Jesus didn't come to condemn the world, but came to seek and to save the lost (John 3:17; 12:47; Luke 19:10). We all start out lost, whether we realize it or not. He became the "go-between," bridging the gap between God and us, to fulfill our desperate need and longing for the perfect Dad we've always wished for.

Every child has a God-given need to be raised and nurtured by a loving father. Without this father role, the child is destined for a troubled life. Consider these findings from the National Center for Fathering:

- 36.3 percent of children live without their biological father.
- The U.S. Department of Health and Human Services states that fatherless children are at a dramatically greater risk of drug and alcohol abuse.
- Children who live apart from their fathers are 4.3 times more likely to smoke cigarettes as teenagers than children growing up with their fathers in the home.
- Three out of four teenage suicides occur in households where a parent has been absent.

These alarming statistics confirm the epidemic of "fatherlessness" in our nation today. Numerous studies have shown that an absentee father drastically affects a child's mental, physical and emotional development, as well as his financial future, sexual behavior and drug and alcohol use. It's unfortunate, but many people hold grudges, even after their fathers have died, for things that happened in their childhood.

In a perfect world, our earthly fathers would be a living example of our heavenly Father's love. We would readily want to run into our heavenly

Dad's arms. Sadly, only a small number of us have had first-hand experience with a earthly father who reflects the qualities of our heavenly Father.

Consequently, God uses the imperfection of our earthly fathers to guide our deep longing into the presence of the only perfect Father, God.

LONGING FOR DAD

Deep down we all yearn for a father who will take an interest in us.

We all silently desire that our father would get to know what we think and feel. We yearn to regularly hear that we're loved—that our dads are proud of us. We want them to know us intimately, to understand us, and even greatly delight in us. We want a father who believes in us and will exuberantly cheer us on, giving us strength that will sustain us later in life. We want our fathers to reassure us that the future ahead is very bright for us.

> *You weren't an accident. You weren't mass-produced. You aren't an assembly-line product. You were deliberately planned, specifically gifted, and lovingly positioned on the Earth by the Master Craftsman.—Max Lucado*

It's important for every father to encourage his son—to tell him he was born to be a mighty warrior; that he is more than a conqueror; that he has the necessary tools to win any battle that comes along; that he can do the impossible because of his unshakeable faith and courage.

Every daughter wants to be daddy's girl. She longs to hear him say that she's his most precious princess—that she's the most beautiful girl in the world. She needs to hear that he'll protect her from all the evil villains in the world.

We all need to believe we'll succeed in whatever challenge that comes along—to know that failure is not the end of the world, to know that our dad will not abandon us or hate us for failing.

Our desperate longing to be loved can only be fulfilled from a loving Dad. This deep longing is what John Eldredge's book, *Wild At Heart*, calls the "father wound" that is found in so many men and boys in our society today.

SEARCHING FOR DAD

There's a story of a father and son in Spain who became estranged, and the son ran away.

After months of searching for his son in vain, the father put a classified ad in a Madrid newspaper that said this: "Dear Paco, meet me in front of this newspaper office at noon on Saturday. All is forgiven. I love you. Your Father." At noon on the following Saturday, 800 Pacos were in front of the newspaper office.

Well, there's good news. Your Dad in heaven knows the longing of your heart! The great God of the universe was the One who created and placed within you this very longing—your internal signal beacon—designed to bring you home to your ultimate Dad. He creatively designed it so all the other God replacements you use to fill the Father-love void within, will fail miserably.

The Creator chose to become like His creatures, and He paid the penalty for our crimes so that as our heavenly Father, He could adopt those who truly trust Him.

> But when the time had fully come, God sent his Son, born of a woman, born under law, to redeem those under law, that we might receive the full rights of sons. Because you are sons, God sent the Spirit of his Son into our hearts, the Spirit who calls out, "Abba, Father." So you are no longer a slave, but a son; and since you are a son, God has made you also an heir. (Galatians 4:4-7)

> You are all sons of God through faith in Christ Jesus. (Galatians 3:26)

During His time on earth, Jesus started a controversial trend when He addressed God as "Abba." This was no different than our calling Him "Daddy" today. But in the first century Jewish culture, calling God "Dad" was considered absolutely unthinkable and irreverent. It expressed a level of intimacy unfamiliar and abhorrent to them.

The apostle Paul, in his letter to the Galatians, repeats this same term—"Abba, Father" (Galatians 4:6). In this context, he says once you belong to Him, you are allowed to call God by the same name Jesus did—Daddy. I love it. What a privilege! God is so much more than a divine ruler. He's the supreme head of a very large family, and He desires to invite spiritual orphans to become a part of His family.

Your heavenly Dad has always been with you. He watched over you even before you were born, and He personally custom designed you with all your unique gifts, talents, and personality traits. He was beside you when your earthly father decided to work, read the newspaper, watch TV, or surf the Internet rather than spend time with you. He was there to cheer you on at your recital, your game, your graduation, even when your earthly father couldn't make it. He was with you every time the tears fell, and you sobbed in your bedroom or on that lonely walk. God's heart broke as He watched your heart break.

Your earthly dad may have abandoned you, but your heavenly Dad will never do so.

Never will I leave you; never will I forsake you. (Hebrews 13:5)

When you pass through the waters, I will be with you; and when you pass through the rivers, they will not sweep over you. When you walk through the fire, you will not be burned; the flames will not set you ablaze. (Isaiah 43:2)

Even as you read this book, your heavenly Dad is watching you with delight, excited that you're finally able to receive the amazing love He's loved you with since the beginning of time. He's very, very different than your earthly dad. He's deeply interested in you, and more than anything else, He wants an intimate relationship with you. You are a highly valued member of His family.

Without faith, it's impossible to make Him happy (Hebrews 11:6). Think about this: He didn't say it's impossible to make Him happy without perfection or complete knowledge. Your Father in heaven knows you believe in Him. He's extremely happy with you. Since happy people smile, you can be certain He looks down from heaven and smiles at you! He never raises His voice at you or frowns at you. He is gracious and compassionate, slow to anger, and "abounding in love" (Psalm 103:8, Exodus 34:6, Nehemiah 9:17, Joel 2:13, Jonah 4:2).

MY CHILDREN

Kristy and I have a precious four-year-old daughter. I am head-over-heels in love with her. She's so much fun. Often she'll come to me during the day and rub my back, giving me the sweetest smile in the world.

We also have a handsome two-year-old son, who I am absolutely crazy about. He is the most captivating little man-child I could wish for. We call him our little preacher because he talks a mile a minute.

It's amazingly fulfilling to have a little princess to cuddle with and a son to play and wrestle with. My children only have one problem with me. I exasperate them with my kisses. They always squirm and squeal for me to stop way before I'm done kissing them.

Every night, I hold them in my arms, look into their eyes, and gently say to each of them, "You are my child, and I love you. I am very happy with you." I remind them that I believe in them and that they will do the impossible because of their faith in God. I remind them that I am extremely proud of who they are.

Now granted, neither one has contributed very much to the family so far. They have yet to make dinner, mow the lawn, make money, or repair anything around the house. So far they're just normal kids, being their precious, unique selves. Nevertheless, I enjoy them enormously and I am absolutely crazy about them, because they are my children. How much more does our God, who is exceedingly more loving than I am, enjoy and delight in those who are *His* children.

> If you, then, though you are evil, know how to give good gifts to your children, how much more will your Father in heaven give good gifts to those who ask him! (Jesus, in Matthew 7:11)

As much as you adore your children, your Dad in heaven is even crazier about you! He wants to be up-close and personal with you—to pierce the dimensional gap so He can hug and hold you, and tell you how much He loves you. And the amazing fact is that He did do this!

He wants you to know that all your mistakes and failures in the past, present and future were deleted, erased from His memory when you received His forgiveness. All God's anger and irritation was unloaded on His only Son two thousand years ago.

God made him who had no sin to be sin for us, so that in him
we might become the righteousness of God. (2 Corinthians 5:21)

Whoever believes in the Son has eternal life, but whoever rejects the
Son will not see life, for God's wrath remains on him. (John 3:36)

Some people use fear to motivate others to obey. Although it's very important to fear and respect God, those are not the reasons that you love Him. Once you belong to Him, you no longer need to be motivated by the dread of His anger. He now delights in you. You're now family!

For you did not receive a spirit that makes you a slave *again to
fear,* but you received the Spirit of sonship. And by him we cry,
"Abba, Father." (Romans 8:15)

As amazing as it sounds, God believes in you and is proud of you. He can't wait to look into your eyes and tell you how much you mean to Him. It's His fervent desire to share with you what's on His heart (See Psalm 25:14). He has never stopped looking at you and delighting in you since the day of your birth (See Psalm 139).

Consider these incredible truths about yourself. You are not an accident. You are unique and original in every way. You were created for a specific and personal mission that no one but you can fulfill. He wants to shower you with His heart's delight.

He who did not spare His own Son, but gave Him up for us all—how will he not also, along with Him, graciously give us all things? (Romans 8:32)

"...how will he not also..." How could you think your heavenly Father desires less than the best for you when He ransomed His child to restore you to Himself? After such a sacrifice, will He now withhold from you? I'm not saying that you will never have pain, disappointments, or tragedy. I'm merely sharing one part of my Father's heart that's rarely talked about.

MY FATHER'S LOVE

When I encountered the Lord Jesus on November 23, 1986, He became my Hero and my Savior, saving me from a miserable life of emptiness and rebellion.

Then He became the friend I never had, and I would share with Him all the tragic drama we create as teenagers. Later I was introduced to the Person of the Holy Spirit, who became my power source and my counselor. But I have to admit, God the Father remained a mystery to me, a forbidding form hidden behind a curtain—a faceless and distant ruler.

It was years ago when I sought to discover the identity of the faceless person behind that mysterious curtain. But in my search I often felt I was flailing in the dark, grasping at smoke. Have you ever felt that way? One day I'd feel really good about being loved by God; the next day I felt distant from Him, like He wasn't around or wasn't truly interested in me.

Then I discovered the Father's Love Letter, a letter written by Barry Adams. I also watched Barry's video, *The Journey Home to Love*. It took my relationship with God to an entirely new level. After watching the video, I ran to my closet and wept like a baby for thirty minutes. I was absolutely broken, deeply moved by the depth of His love. I could hardly believe how much God has wanted to be my Dad.

Below is the letter written by Barry Adams, based on what God said in the Bible:

My child,

You may not know me, but I know everything about you. *Psalm 139:1*

I know when you sit down and when you rise up. *Psalm 139:2*

I am familiar with all your ways. *Psalm 139:3*

Even the very hairs on your head are numbered. *Matthew 10:29-31*

For you were made in my image. *Genesis 1:27*

In me you live and move and have your being. *Acts 17:28*

For you are my offspring. *Acts 17:28*

I knew you even before you were conceived. *Jeremiah 1:4-5*

I chose you when I planned creation. *Ephesians 1:11-12*

You were not a mistake, for all your days are written in my book. *Psalm 139:15-16*

I determined the exact time of your birth and where you would live. *Acts 17:26*

You are fearfully and wonderfully made. *Psalm 139:14*

I knit you together in your mother's womb. *Psalm 139:13*

And brought you forth on the day you were born. *Psalm 71:6*

I have been misrepresented by those who don't know me. *John 8:41-44*

I am not distant and angry, but am the complete expression of love. *1 John 4:16*

And it is my desire to lavish my love on you. *1 John 3:1*

Simply because you are my child and I am your Father. *1 John 3:1*

I offer you more than your earthly father ever could. *Matthew 7:11*

For I am the perfect father. *Matthew 5:48*

Every good gift that you receive comes from my hand. *James 1:17*

For I am your provider and I meet all your needs.
Matthew 6:31-33

My plan for your future has always been filled with hope.
Jeremiah 29:11

Because I love you with an everlasting love. *Jeremiah 31:3*

My thoughts toward you are countless as the sand on the seashore. *Psalm 139:17-18*

And I rejoice over you with singing. *Zephaniah 3:17*

I will never stop doing good to you. *Jeremiah 32:40*

For you are my treasured possession. *Exodus 19:5*

I desire to establish you with all my heart and all my soul.
Jeremiah 32:41

And I want to show you great and marvelous things.
Jeremiah 33:3

If you seek me with all your heart, you will find me.
Deuteronomy 4:29

Delight in me and I will give you the desires of your heart.
Psalm 37:4

For it is I who gave you those desires. *Philippians 2:13*

I am able to do more for you than you could possibly imagine.
Ephesians 3:20

For I am your greatest encourager. *2 Thessalonians 2:16-17*

I am also the Father who comforts you in all your troubles.
2 Corinthians 1:3-4

When you are brokenhearted, I am close to you.
Psalm 34:18

As a shepherd carries a lamb, I have carried you close to my heart. *Isaiah 40:11*

One day I will wipe away every tear from your eyes.
Revelation 21:3-4

And I'll take away all the pain you have suffered on this earth. *Revelation 21:3-4*

I am your Father, and I love you even as I love my son, Jesus.
John 17:23
For in Jesus, my love for you is revealed. *John 17:26*
He is the exact representation of my being. *Hebrews 1:3*
He came to demonstrate that I am for you, not against you.
Romans 8:31
And to tell you that I am not counting your sins.
2 Corinthians 5:18-19
Jesus died so that you and I could be reconciled.
2 Corinthians 5:18-19
His death was the ultimate expression of my love for you.
1 John 4:10
I gave up everything I loved that I might gain your love.
Romans 8:31-32
If you receive the gift of my son Jesus, you receive me.
1 John 2:23
And nothing will ever separate you from my love again.
Romans 8:38-39
Come home and I'll throw the biggest party heaven has ever
seen. *Luke 15:7*
I have always been Father, and will always be Father.
Ephesians 3:14-15
My question is...Will you be my child? *John 1:12-13*
I am waiting for you. *Luke 15:11-32*
Love,
Your Dad, Almighty God[1]

Once I grabbed hold of my Dad's incredible love, it only increased my appreciation for my earthly father. At that moment, old un-met needs suddenly faded into insignificance, and I could fully release my dad from my expectations of perfection.

---

1. Father's Love Letter, Barry Adams

Is He Your Dad?

How do you know if you've truly received the Father's love? Is there a biblical test to know whether you have truly experienced this, or is it merely information in your head?

These passages tell you how you can know:

The only thing that counts is faith expressing itself through love. (Galatians 5:6)

We know that we have passed out of death to life, because we love our brothers. Anyone who does not love remains in death... Everyone who loves has been born of God and knows God. Whoever does not love does not know God, because God is love... If anyone says, "I love God," yet hates his brother, he is a liar. For anyone who does not love his brother, whom he has seen, cannot love God, whom he has not seen... If anyone obeys his word, God's love is truly made complete in him. This is how we know we are in him. (1 John 3:14; 4:7, 4:8; 4:20; 2:5)

According to these verses, there are only two possible outcomes:
1. You will love others, if you've experienced and believed God's love for you.
2. You will not love others, if you haven't experienced or received God's love.

This, in a nutshell, is the *Indebtedness Principle* at work. Of course, most people find themselves somewhere in between these two extremes. Nevertheless, these are two logical conclusions that the book of 1 John trumpets without apology. Just pause for a few minutes and consider these questions:

Do you struggle to be patient and forgiving toward others?

Do you have trouble listening and taking an interest in other people's lives?

Is it hard for you to serve, give and truly encourage others?

If you answered yes to these questions, there's a strong probability you haven't received God's love. If you had, you would love other people. Remember, the solution in this case is not to try harder, but to dig deeper. You live out what you believe about God.

Those who always correct others believe God is always rebuking and correcting them; but those who believe God hears, understands, encourages and empowers them will be busy doing those same things for others. In order to love, you must learn to receive God's love first.

Those people who became personally involved with Jesus were never the same again. They shared the gospel, not because they had to do it out of guilt, but because they were compelled to *after* receiving His great love.

When they saw the courage of Peter and John and realized that they were unschooled, ordinary men, they were astonished and they took note that these men had been with Jesus... Then they called them in again and commanded them not to speak or teach at all in the name of Jesus. But Peter and John replied, "Judge for yourselves whether it is right in God's sight to obey you rather than God. For we cannot help speaking about what we have seen and heard." (Acts 4:13, 18-20)

On Judgment Day, many will be surprised that they never truly knew God.

Imagine a man walking up to a woman and telling her he knows her name, phone number, address and social security number. Then imagine him smiling and proposing marriage. Obviously, most women would respond by saying, "I don't know where you got this information, but I wouldn't even dream of marrying someone I didn't know."

Imagine the man replying, "I can't believe you won't marry me! I know so much about you. Do you know I mowed your lawn and went grocery shopping for you yesterday? I even wrote a song for you! How can you not want to marry me? I've done so much for you."

She most likely would respond with, "I don't know you. Leave me alone!"

How horrible it will be for those who think they're Christians, only to be devastated when Jesus drops this bomb on them on Judgment Day. At that moment, they'll regret simply following rules and studying facts about Him, but never really pursuing Him in a personal way. They tried to live the "Christian life," based on what they knew about God, but they never had a personal relationship with Him.

> Not everyone who says to me, "Lord, Lord," will enter the kingdom of heaven… Many will say to me that day, "Lord, Lord, did we not prophesy in Your name, and in Your name drive out demons and perform many miracles?" Then I will tell them plainly, "I never knew you. Away from me, you evildoers!"
> (Matthew 7:21-23)

> This will happen when the Lord Jesus is revealed from heaven in blazing fire with His powerful angels. He will punish those who do not know God and do not obey the gospel of our Lord Jesus. They will be punished with everlasting destruction…
> (2 Thessalonians 1:7-9)

Love, courage and faith are not simply a list of character qualities you "work on" and check off one at a time. They result from an intimate encounter with Christ. In truth, the twelve disciples were really very ordinary men who were radically transformed by the greatest and most loving Hero the world has ever seen.

Many people fall into the exhausting trap of just trying harder to love others.

In the next chapter, you'll learn how you can not only know the Father's love in your head, but also experience it in your heart. You'll also learn how to finally break the false and crippling association between your earthly dad and your Heavenly Dad.

SUMMARY

1. Jesus summarized your purpose statement: to love God and to love others as yourself.
2. You love God and others because He first loved you (the *Indebtedness Principle*).
3. God adopted you so He could be the Dad you've always wished for.
4. Your earthly dad's imperfections cause you to look for the perfect Dad—God.
5. The biblical test of whether or not you know God is your love for others.

DISCUSSION QUESTIONS

1. Do you have difficulty receiving praise or gifts?
2. How do you see God the Father? Do you see Him as your Dad?
3. When you think of God, what is His facial expression as He looks at you?

PRAYER

Lord, help me to increasingly grasp the depth of Your love.
Teach me to see and receive Your love throughout the day.
I desire to love You more, so please continually pour out love into
my heart for You. Help me to understand the fact that You are
the perfect Dad I've always wanted. Thank You, Lord!

CHAPTER 5

OVERCOMING STRESS

Understanding and Mastering Your Mind and Heart

*Thoughts lead on to purposes; purposes go forth in action;
actions form habits; habits decide character;
and character fixes our destiny.*
—TYRON EDWARDS

*Creating a joint venture between head and heart
puts a power pack behind your goals.*
—DOC CHILDRE

Have you ever wondered why so many of us give up on New Year's resolutions?

When you try to change your behavior rather than your belief system, the result is only a temporary change at best. Attempting to change habits using your will power alone is like putting a Band-Aid on a broken bone. Most dieting doesn't work for this same reason.

THE SECRET KEY

Imagine being handed a large, foot-long key. It's shiny and golden.

Can you feel how heavy and smooth it is? You close your hand around the key and squeeze it. You feel the excitement as you are led to a secret door. You are consumed with anticipation, wondering what you might possibly discover behind that door.

As you slip the key into the lock and carefully turn it, the door creaks open and light streams into a place long hidden. What precious treasures have been concealed here? In the shadows you can make out the outline of a treasure chest full of truths—truths that will help you overcome stress and empower you to live the promised abundant life.

Though you may not have realized it, you've had access to this key all your life. You also discover that everyone else has had access to the same key, though few seem to put it to use.

The only thing you have the ability to control is your mind.

This key is God's gift to you. This gift is *the choice to control your mind.*

World-famous author and public speaker, Dale Carnegie, was once asked what he thought was the greatest thing he'd ever learned. He said,

> By far the most important lesson I have ever learned is the importance of what we think. If I knew what you think, I would know what you are. Our thoughts make us what we are. Our mental attitude is the x-factor that determines our faith. Emerson said a man is what he thinks about all day long. How could he possibly be anything else? I know now with a conviction beyond all doubt that the biggest problem you and I have to deal with is choosing the right thought. If we can do that we will be on the high road to solving all of our problems. The great philosopher who ruled the Roman Empire, Marcus Aurelius, summed it up in eight words, "Our life is what our thoughts make it."

If you desire to truly grasp the depth of God's love and the fact that He delights in you, you need to understand how your mind works in relation to your heart, your spirit and your belief system.

Many would list the keys to successful Christian living as follows: the Holy Spirit, Bible study, prayer and church involvement. I wholeheartedly agree. But you must first understand and manage all of these keys within your mind. When you understand that the only thing you have the ability to control is your mind, you can then be responsible to implement every other biblical "key" to your life.

WHAT IS THE "HEART?"

Have you ever wondered what the Bible means when it talks about the heart?

We all know it's not referring to the blood-pumping organ inside the chest. When we speak about the heart, we often are referring to our desires, feelings, memories, fears and opinions.

So what is the "heart"—that part of us that carries all these things?

The term "heart" represents what today has become generally known to experts as the subconscious mind. The conscious mind makes up ten percent of the total mind, and the subconscious the remaining ninety percent. The subconscious is the storehouse for all our desires, feelings, memories, fears and opinions. Unlike the conscious mind, it never sleeps.

Acting as a hard drive that stores information fed to it by the conscious mind, the subconscious lacks the capacity to reason or make choices. Its exclusive job is to obey what the conscious mind commands. The conscious mind is the captain of this mental ship.

Interestingly, if there's ever an argument between the conscious and the subconscious mind, guess who wins the argument? No question—the subconscious mind rules the day! This is evidenced by the fact that, as studies show, almost all buying decisions are emotionally based. In essence, when we speak of our "mind and heart," we're referring to the two different sections of the mind, each having its own distinct role.

Following are Scripture verses that refer to our heart. It's interesting to read them now that we know what the heart is:

> But the LORD said to Samuel, "Do not consider his appearance or his height, for I have rejected him. The LORD does not look at the things man looks at. Man looks at the outward appearance, but the LORD looks at the heart." (1 Samuel 16:7)

> Love the LORD your God with all your heart and with all your soul and with all your strength. (Deuteronomy 6:5)

How Your Heart Works

All of your experiences are recorded in your heart.

Your ability to manage your heart, as opposed to choosing to deny your feelings, determines how well you will process your memories and whether you will interpret your past from the standpoint of faith or the standpoint of a victim. Every picture from the past—pleasant or traumatic—is stored in the heart.

In the Old Testament, a man by the name of Joseph was violently assaulted by his own brothers, abandoned, left for dead in a pit and unjustly imprisoned for thirteen years. How would you have interpreted your memories had this been your story?

Joseph could have chosen the role of a victim. He could have become bitter, self-preserving or fearful. Instead, he desperately ran to and trusted in the One who was in charge of all things. He chose to interpret his past through the lens of faith in the One who intended good toward him. He was able to tell his brothers, "You intended to harm me, but God intended it for good to accomplish what is now being done, the saving of many lives" (Genesis 50:20). *Intended* is a word clarifying God's motive of love behind this event.

Repetitious truth thinking and reinterpreting your past through the lens of faith and forgiveness is how you are to finally break the false and crippling association between your earthly dad and your Heavenly Dad.

For the most part, when I find myself in situations that bring fear into my life, I realize that the fear is only revealing past experiences I never dealt with. Thank God that He makes all things new! Now, when these situations reveal the pain I experienced in the past, I say to my Lord: "Thank You that I am no longer that person who was afraid or angry with that (situation or person). Today, I choose to forgive and act courageously! I know that your loving and powerful hand is behind everything that has happened in my life."

When you wallow in fear and bitterness, your heart begins to create false associations with both the past and the present. Here are some examples:

- A dog viciously attacked Harold when he was very young. Ever since, he hasn't wanted anything to do with dogs, including little yappers.
- Katie had a big brother who was continually finding fault with her while she was growing up. As an adult, she became closed-minded when faced with any conflicts. Now, she projects the anger she felt toward her brother onto anyone in authority over her.
- Jerry grew up with a controlling mom who had the tendency to micromanage his life. When he married, he began to overreact to his wife's suggestions. Jerry's bitterness toward his mom caused him to be overly sensitive and defensive with his wife.
- Sheri's dad was non-communicative. When at home, he spent most of his time watching television and reading the newspaper. Because he failed to initiate a relationship with Sheri, she now rejects God because she believes He, too, is a distant and uncaring Father.

Every overreaction simply reflects the hurt that is buried in your heart. Stuffed down fear and bitterness will inevitably surface. In reality, circumstances don't break you, they just reveal who you really are inside. Conflicts always trigger unresolved fear and bitterness from the past. The issue at hand is rarely the real issue. All of your fears, bitterness and strongly held beliefs take up residence in your heart.

Every overreaction simply reflects the hurt that is buried in your heart.

For out of the heart come evil thoughts, murder, adultery, sexual immorality, theft, false testimony, slander. (Jesus, in Matthew 15:19)

BELIEF ABOUT BELIEFS

A belief is a thought you accept as true, whether or not it really is. A thought begins in the conscious mind, but as time allows the thought to marinate, it ends up in the heart. Your belief system resides in the heart, not in the conscious mind. It is the result of the repetition of thoughts you have chosen. The repetition of a thought, supported by certain experiences and observations you've made (reasonable or not), produces a belief.

By the age of thirteen or fourteen, your mental programming regarding marriage, finances and relationships have been set in your subconscious mind. As adults, your life is the evidence, or the printouts, so to speak, of the mental programming you've received up to that point.

Dr. Stephen Kraus, a scientist from Harvard University, discovered after interviewing numerous extremely successful people that the one key to success is belief. "Belief," he says, "is a powerful predictor of success." He understands that our belief always determines our actions.

So what exactly happens with your mind and brain when it comes to forming beliefs?

THE MIND-BRAIN CONNECTION

From a purely spiritual viewpoint, growing a loving relationship with the beautiful God of the universe is best done by:

1. Reading the Bible and talking with Him
2. Dependence on and assistance from the Holy Spirit
3. Being underneath the covering of a local church

From a purely scientific and human viewpoint, what happens to you when we get involved in the activities listed above? All three originate and are processed within your spirit, conscious mind and heart.

Through the years, I have observed that many Christians go to seminars and camps. As one who has also participated in these kinds of events, one of the questions that continually runs through my mind is: "Why are the results of these events short lived? What's the key to long term and permanent change?" Based on my studies of the Bible, supported by scientific evidence, the key to long-term change is repetition of truthful thinking that produces truthful beliefs within the context of a relationship with your heavenly Dad.

Truthful beliefs will always produce the promised abundant life. Lies always produce stress.

Allow me to illustrate how the brain is affected by the mind's repetitious thinking of truth.

My four-year-old daughter loves to learn. Let's examine what happens in her brain during the learning process.

The brain is made up of billions of nerve cells called neurons. Every time my daughter learns something new, a baby neuron or nerve cell is born. This process is known as neurogenesis. When she learns more about a subject, tiny branches called dendrites grow and spread out from the neurons and connect and communicate with other neurons through synapses. The more frequently she hears about what she's learned, the more her dendrites grow. The more her dendrites spread inside her brain, the more her brainpower increases.

Now that you've seen how your brain develops as you process new information and the resulting emotions, let me illustrate how your mind changes from believing a lie to believing truth.

Dr. Martell grew up thinking the earth was flat. That thought was contained in a neuron inside his brain. Since he has believed this most of his life, the dendrites on this neuron were quite vast with their branches intricately spread throughout his brain.

Now let's say you went to Dr. Martell and told him the earth was round. You provided pictures, detailed videos and testimonies from renowned scientists. Because this is so contrary to his deeply held personal convictions, he will probably experience some intense emotional shock. Since the evidence was too conclusive to ignore, he makes the decision to believe this newfound discovery once he gets past his initial surprise. As a result of believing this new truth, a baby neuron starts to grow inside his brain, and with continued thinking, an aggressive web of dendrites will gradually spread. Every week for the next year, Martell reads articles on the subject, educating himself more and more. This constant reminder helps develop the widespread growth of his dendrites, imbedding his belief deeply. It's unlikely that Martell could ever be convinced by anyone that the earth is flat. That old flat-earth neuron has withered long ago, and has been replaced by the new.

Dendrites follow the use-it-or-lose-it rule. Think a thought once and your dendrite won't last. Think it over and over again for a long period of time, and the neural network in your brain grows like a spider's web. This is how belief systems develop in your brain. Dendrites have a half-life of fourteen days. When you don't repeat a thinking process within fourteen days after first learning a new idea, half of the dendrites wither. Fourteen days later, they die by half again. This is why there are so many books available that claim you can break or form a habit in thirty days.

Now, you're probably asking, "How does this have anything to do with God?"

God is the One who designed your brain and He knows that if you don't implement daily habits of remembering, truth dendrites begin to shrivel and die. Did you know that in Deuteronomy alone, the word *remember* is mentioned seventeen times? The same admonition to remember is repeated over and over throughout the Bible:

Remember how the LORD your God led you all the way in the desert these forty years, to humble you and to test you in order to know what was in your heart, whether or not you would keep his commands. (Deuteronomy 8:2)

But remember the LORD your God, for it is he who gives you the ability to produce wealth, and so confirms his covenant, which he swore to your forefathers, as it is today. (Deuteronomy 8:18)

Only be careful, and watch yourselves closely so that you do not forget the things your eyes have seen or let them slip from your heart as long as you live. (Deuteronomy 4:9)

> *We are what we repeatedly do.—Aristotle*

When you are not daily remembering God, your mind will unavoidably accept lies from the overwhelming voice of the world. Beginning in the next chapter, you'll learn in more detail the 7 habits that you will be implementing to *remember* your God and dramatically grow your truth dendrites.

MIND MISMANAGEMENT PRODUCES STRESS

Your conscious mind is the gatekeeper of your heart.

It's the manager, programmer and bodyguard of your heart. The conscious mind makes the choice to correct the lie your heart believes with the truth of God's Word. This explains why the Bible says it's so critical that you protect your heart: "Above all else, guard your heart, for it is the wellspring of life" (Proverbs 4:23).

When you choose not to take responsibility for your thoughts, stress happens.

During his work at Stanford Medical School, renowned cellular biologist Dr. Bruce Lipton concluded that stress is caused by false beliefs. In other words, lies cause stress. As mentioned earlier, lies cause fear and bitterness, which eventually causes stress.

Stress activates your body's emergency alarm system, producing a very toxic and dangerous hormone called cortisol. Your bodies were designed to tolerate up to twenty-five grams of cortisol per day. The problem is that the "what if" thinking pushes the cortisol levels way over that limit:

- What if my husband dies on his way home from work?
- What if my boss fires me?
- What if I can't make my car payment next week?
- What if I fail my next test?

All those fictitious fear-based thoughts cause stress and release cortisol into your bloodstream. Cortisol slowly destroys the white blood cells and other necessary cancer-fighting cells in your immune system. Cortisol interferes with the body's natural ability to heal itself. Stress is to your body what termites are to a house. It slowly but surely eats you to death.

The immune system is like a chain made up of links. Illness and disease are waiting to rain down on your immune system and will find the weakest link to attack the path of least resistance. Designed to protect you from illness, the immune system struggles under the destructive effects of stress, as proven by hundreds of research studies.

Most people who choose to live a life of fear and bitterness, destroy their immune system and become ill. What's sad is some have mistakenly blamed the cause of their illness on heredity, the environment, demonic influence, old age or bad luck. Though there are definitely exceptions, and it's clear that not everyone who's ill lives a stressed life, it is inevitable that those who do suffer with stress suffer physically.

I strongly encourage an open-minded approach to this subject and a willingness to research the connection of stress (whether as a cause or aggravation) to almost every illness—depression, cancer, asthma, allergies, heart disease, lupus, arthritis, insomnia, obesity, etc.

> *The tendency to avoid problems and the emotional suffering inherent in them is the primary basis of all human mental illness.—M. Scott Peck*

Stress, society's code word for fear and bitterness, is the primary killer today. According to the Center for Disease Control, eighty three percent of all deaths of adults between twenty-one and sixty-five are related to lifestyle and stress. It has in many cases become so much a way of life that it isn't clearly recognized, or it is simply denied.

It is imperative to become reconciled to God, others and yourself, rather than simply medicating your hidden and silent misery with a deathly array of emotional anesthetics.

The sorrows of those will increase who run after other gods. (Psalm 16:4)

EMOTIONAL ANESTHETICS FOR THE HEART

As mentioned earlier, our society offers an abundance of emotional anesthetics to aid in the attempt to relieve stress, instead of finding our rest in the God of rest Himself.

A most popular and dangerous God-replacement (idol) today is television. The interesting thing about TV is that your subconscious mind is not able to determine what is real or true and what isn't. It views everything it sees as reality and truth, which explains why you become emotionally affected while watching a show or a movie.

Multiple studies have proven that watching TV is mostly a subconscious experience, which is literally identical to being hypnotized. The viewer could go from a normal state of mind to a hypnotized mental state within thirty seconds when watching television. The mind is left vulnerable to be brainwashed by whatever message it hears and sees. What does the Bible say about this?

Do not bring a detestable thing into your house or you, like it, will be set apart for destruction... I will set before my eyes no vile thing. (Deuteronomy 7:26, Psalm 101:3)

Have you ever wondered why watching TV is so addictive? While you're watching TV, your brain releases a chemical called dopamine. Dopamine is the "feel good" hormone released by the pituitary gland into your bloodstream, the same hormone released through these other activities:

- listening to your favorite music
- using drugs: alcohol, cocaine and tobacco
- eating/drinking
- sexual orgasm
- accomplishing a task from your to-do list
- playing video games
- watching movies

Interestingly, all the above activities have a tendency to become addictive. And every addiction is rooted in the need to be loved. Addiction is a form of slavery when you choose a counterfeit and deceptive promise of feeding your hunger to be loved. It's the pursuit of temporary pleasure (dopamine rush) to silence the cries of your heart to be loved. Phillip Yancey has said, "what the Old Testament calls idolatry, enlightened Westerners call 'addiction.'"

My people have committed two sins: they have turned from Me, the living water, and dug their own cisterns, broken cisterns that cannot hold water. (Jeremiah 2:13)

How many times have you watched TV, only to be left empty and wanting more after you turn it off? There's always an emotional dip that occurs after you've left the fantasy world you wished you lived in. It's the alternative escape from your painful, present condition.

Every addiction is rooted in the need to be loved.

There's nothing inherently evil in these activities mentioned above. The motive and reason for taking part in these activities is what makes it idolatry. Addiction is a condition of the heart.

Satan's goal for you is a cluttered mind. If you live without the power of solitude and the reflective thinking that results, you turn into mental zombies.

I remember when I used to anxiously look forward to a vacation to escape my stress. Since then, I've learned that even if I spent a month in Hawaii, my problems would still find me. They reside inside of me. A vacation, then, needs to happen within me, in the rest and peace that originate in a trusting relationship with my heavenly Dad.

You have filled my heart with greater joy than when their grain and new wine abound… The LORD is my strength and my shield; my heart trusts in him, and I am helped. My heart leaps for joy and I will give thanks to him in song… I will go to the altar of God, to God, my joy and my delight… Satisfy us in the morning with your unfailing love, that we may sing for joy and be glad all our days. (Psalms 4:7; 28:7; 43:4; 90:14)

RESTING IN GOD

Stress is the result of trying to control something that's uncontrollable. You try to control a situation or a relational outcome because you fear the outcome will be the opposite of what you want. More often than not, you have this fear because you've believed a lie.

This is the reason the Bible says to repent, which literally means *to change your thinking.* Because God is your rest, you don't have to believe lies that stress you out. He wants you to receive the enormity of His love toward you. He is your rest. You don't ever have to find "relaxation" in a thousand different sources to relieve your stress.

> Do you not know? Have you not heard? The LORD is the ever-lasting God, the Creator of the ends of the earth. He will not grow tired or weary, and his understanding no one can fathom. He gives strength to the weary and increases the power of the weak. Even youths grow tired and weary, and young men stumble and fall; but those who hope in the LORD will renew their strength. They will soar on wings like eagles; they will run and not grow weary, they will walk and not be faint. (Isaiah 40:28-31)

To "hope in the Lord" (Isaiah 40:31) is a mind-heart decision and a choice. The result is that you'll have unexpected and supernatural strength!

I have personally experienced this amazing unexpected strength. In the past, I had chronic fatigue syndrome and hypoglycemia. I needed food at least every three hours to keep my blood-sugar levels up. As I've gotten to know my Lord on a deeper level, I've experienced energy beyond what I ever thought was possible. In addition, I got to a point where I was able to fast!

I have read countless scientific studies citing cases involving people who were healed from every known disease out there. If you are struggling with an illness or an addiction, you have hope! Please believe that God is more powerful and loving than you could possibly ever imagine.

Years before my own personal breakthrough, a friend of mine, Sean, told me his story. He was healed from a ten-year struggle with Multiple Chemical Sensitivity (MCS). I remembered thinking at the time, *Good for you, but not for me.* I was too closed-hearted to even consider the possibility that the mind-body connection applied to my life.

Awhile later, things in my life started to change, for the worse. After having experienced many years of considerable stability and financial success, we faced a two-year period of upheaval. I had four different jobs, moved five times, lost a close loved one and lost all of the equity from our real estate properties. We also lost thousands of dollars in a real estate venture and became buried in debt. In addition, we had the responsibility of caring for our two young children.

This was the stressful context that set the stage for the birth of this book.

It was during this difficult time that Kristy and I had asked the question, "Isn't there more to Christianity than this?" There was no doubt that God had placed this deep hunger we were experiencing in our hearts. This was the beginning of an aggressive quest through biblical, medical and scientific research.

Our lives haven't been the same since.

The interesting thing is, the joy and peace we began to experience had nothing to do with the distressing situation we were in! In fact, our difficult circumstances gave us the perfect context to get closer to our God. We experienced many miracles during this time—the kinds of things that we used to think happened only to "other" people.

We've begun the exciting journey to the promised abundant life. Abundant life is not a life-promise for comfort, even though I have no problem with comfort. Abundant life is strength in the midst of trials; wisdom in the midst of confusion; peace in the midst of turmoil; joy in the midst of tragedy; and most of all intimacy with my God in the midst of difficulties.

REPROGRAMMING YOUR MIND'S HARD DRIVE

Did you know the Bible repeats seventy-five times the command to reprogram your mind?

The word *repentance* is used in the Bible to convey the original meaning of changing one's mind. The Bible teaches that the first step to following Jesus is to change your thinking. Change your mind from what? From lies you have unsuspectingly believed. Deuteronomy is adamant about the consequences that will occur if you don't.

> However, if you do not obey the LORD your God and do not carefully follow all his commands and decrees I am giving you today all these curses will come upon you and overtake you... The LORD will send on you curses, confusion and rebuke in everything you put your hand to... The LORD will plague you with diseases until he has destroyed you...The LORD will afflict you with madness, blindness and confusion of mind. (Deuteronomy 28:15,20-21,28)

In other words:

1. If you love Him, you will obey Him.
2. When you don't obey, it's because you don't love Him.
3. The reason you don't love Him is that you believe the lie that He doesn't love you.
4. These lies cause fear and bitterness.
5. Fear and bitterness cause emotional distress also known as stress.
6. Stress destroys your immune system.
7. When your immune system breaks down, it can't fight illness and disease effectively.

The best and only way to reprogram your mind is not by simply eliminating all the lies you believe, but to replace them. This is the power of the *Replacement Principle*. The smartest way to take a bone out of a dog's mouth is not by grabbing it and playing tug-of-war. It's by dropping a fat and juicy porterhouse steak in front of him.

Don't eliminate, replace.

> *Feed your faith, and your fear will starve to death. Fear knocked at the door. Faith answered. No one was there. Fear and faith cannot keep house together; when one enters, the other departs.—Vern McLellan*

The truth that reprograms your mind occurs in the *context* of your relationship with God. The more you spend time with Him, the more your thinking will gradually transform.

Do not conform any longer to the pattern of this world, but be transformed by the renewing of your mind. (Romans 12:2)

Fix these words of mine in your hearts and minds; tie them as symbols on your hands and bind them on your foreheads. Teach them to your children, talking about them when you sit at home and when you walk along the road, when you lie down and when you get up. (Deuteronomy 11:18-19)

In the remainder of this book you will be applying all that you learned in the last five chapters. You will be discovering the seven habits to overcome stress and live the promised abundant life. This is where you'll really see the changes begin in your life!

SUMMARY

1. Your thoughts control how you live your life.
2. Your "heart" is your subconscious mind.

3. Beliefs are thoughts deemed to be true.
4. Repetition grows dendrites in your brain.
5. Stress in your mind affects your body.
6. "Emotional anesthetics" are society's response to stress.
7. Throughout the Bible, God tells you to change your thinking.

DISCUSSION QUESTIONS

1. How have you seen stress affect your body?
2. How have you seen repetitious thoughts play out in your life?
3. Do you use "emotional anesthetics" in your life? What are they?

PRAYER

Thank You so much, Lord, that You've given me the gift
of the choice to control my thinking. I humble myself before You.
Help me take action instead of merely gathering information.
Open my eyes to any lies I have believed without realizing it.
Help me deepen my relationship with You and with others.

PART TWO

7 Habits to Overcome Stress and Live the Promised Abundant Life

CHAPTER 6

KNOWING AND LOVING GOD

The Single Most Important Relationship

Watch your thoughts, for they become words.
Watch your words, for they become actions.
Watch your actions, for they become habits.
Watch your habits, for they become character.
Watch your character, for it becomes your destiny.
—ANONYMOUS

As a nail is driven out by another nail,
habit is overcome by habit.
—LATIN PROVERB

Love *always* starts with God.
Love is not something that you can muster up and distribute. You don't have the capacity or the tendency to draw out any love from within you. None. Your cup is empty. You are not only empty of love, you are desperately longing to *be* loved.

As we covered in chapter four, Jesus took the initiative in reconciling you with your loving heavenly Dad. He first loved you; therefore you treat yourself with the same love that He treated you with. This will result in loving others. When you are separated from God, others and yourself, you will live a life of fear and bitterness, which results in stress. Stress produces cortisol, which in turn destroys your body.

Ever wonder what happens to your body when you truly receive God's love?

When you look at a picture of your sweetheart, anticipating the warm company of the love of your life, dopamine is released in your brain. This is the same hormone released with all the addictions (God-replacements) that we covered in the last chapter. Your body also releases a hormone called oxytocin when you feel loved by someone. Oxytocin has been nicknamed the "bonding" or "cuddle" hormone. You produce it naturally when you love and are loved. Studies have also shown that oxytocin causes a substantial increase in trust among humans.

Studies have shown that oxytocin reduces fear; speeds healing to your body; reduces cravings for addiction; calms you down; eases depression; increases sexual receptivity; counteracts the effects of cortisol; and strengthens your immune system, among many other benefits.

Could you imagine living a life completely believing the truth of God's love for you? Did you know that being in the company of the most loving being in the universe is both addictive and healthy?

Could you imagine living a life completely believing the truth of God's love for you?

It's how your body works according to science! A person either lives in love or in fear. There is no third option. The Bible and neurobiology agree. First John 4:18 says that perfect love (oxytocin) drives out all fear (cortisol).

In the same way that a vehicle could never run on apple juice since it was designed to run on gasoline, your body was designed by God to break down when it's not running on God and His love. By the same token, your body runs efficiently and with supernatural power when you are operating out of God's love continually. It doesn't matter what you say, your body never lies. Your body is a truth machine. I have personally experienced both sides of the fence on this.

No wonder God gives us numerous physical cause-and-effect promises like these:

Do you not know? Have you not heard? The LORD is the everlasting God, the Creator of the ends of the earth. He will not grow tired or weary, and his understanding no one can fathom.

He gives strength to the weary and increases the power of the weak. Even youths grow tired and weary, and young men stumble and fall; but those who hope in the LORD will renew their strength. They will soar on wings like eagles; they will run and not grow weary, they will walk and not be faint. (Isaiah 40:28-31)

I trust and pray that the following chapters will open up your heart so that you would be addicted to His loving presence, that you would no longer see His friendship as a burden.

POWER OF HABITS

Your life equals the sum total of your habits.

Habits are typically acquired from the influence of parents, siblings, friends, or your culture. Leading psychologists tell us that up to ninety percent of our behaviors are habitual. Everything you're going through today is the result of habits you acquired in the past.

Your habits, with no exception, determine the outcome of your life. Habits always deliver results, whether productive or destructive, though the results sometimes don't show up until years later. Both healthy and damaging habits can have a residual influence for hundreds of generations. Habits manifest themselves through action. The one characteristic that separates overcomers from victims is that overcomers take action.

If you truly desire an intimate relationship with your Maker and long to serve Him, you need to respect the power of habits. You need to develop habits that achieve your objectives.

The previous chapters were designed to bring understanding and motivation, while the upcoming chapters will offer encouragement and a challenge for you to take action. In this chapter, I will call you out of the stands to play in the biggest game called Life. We'll be covering the subject of habits that produce *wins* in your life. Now would be a good time to go grab a pen and a pad of paper, along with your schedule or calendar, because, as someone once said, *you'll never cross the ocean by staring at the water.*

Studies have shown that the average Olympian trains about three to five hours a day for six years before competing. All things being equal, the athlete who trained more often typically will outperform the one who didn't train as much.

Even though you may never become an Olympian, you can become a world-class child, servant and warrior for God. The first step in having success in your life journey is to understand and believe that success begins as a spark of thought in the mind. You will learn seven habits that are based on proven principles from the most powerful and best selling book of all time, the Bible, backed by scientific research studies. Together they make up the vehicle that will take you to your destination, and help you achieve your ultimate purpose of developing loving relationships.

IMPLEMENTING THE 7 HABITS

Studies have shown that implementing more than one habit at a time is planned failure. Don't plan on implementing all seven habits at once! I can't emphasize this enough. Your brain is much more efficient when you focus all your energy to form just one habit at a time.

When you first learned how to brush your teeth, you had to be reminded on a regular basis to brush. Today, you have acquired that habit. You do it automatically, like eating, showering, or riding a bike. You don't even think about whether you would brush your teeth or not, you just do.

Implementing more than one habit at a time is planned failure.

Studies have shown, as we covered in chapter four, that it takes about thirty to forty-five days to successfully acquire a habit so that it's firmly cemented in your mind and heart.

To this end, focus all your energy on implementing and praying over one habit at a time:

Schedule it—If it's not on your schedule, it won't get done. This is the first and most important step.

Write it Down—Post it all over your house and car, as well as on your computer.

Leverage it—Find a partner to help you. Accountability is crucial and virtually mandatory in ensuring your success while implementing these habits.

Memorize a verse—Memorize one or two verses that correspond with the habit.

Checkpoints—Put it on your calendar to remind yourself of your new habits, after thirty, ninety and 365 days.

Now it's time to fasten your seatbelt, and make sure you're touching base with the Holy Spirit. You will be implementing seven habits, which will make this a seven-month campaign to abundant life.

⚜

PRAYER

Thank You so much, Lord, that You've given me the choice
to control my thinking. I humble myself before You.
Help me to not just be a reader but one who takes action
with what You will tell me through this book. Please speak to me,
Holy Spirit, that I would never be the same after reading the seven habits.

CHAPTER 7

HABIT #1: FORGIVE

Releasing Yourself

Resentment is like drinking poison
and expecting someone else to die.
—NELSON MANDELA

The hatred you're carrying is a live coal in your heart—
far more damaging to yourself than them.
—LAWANA BLACKWELL

What is really at stake when you don't forgive?

The word *forgive* means "to excuse for a fault or an offense; to cancel from payment; to stop being angry about something."

Imagine discovering one day that you've been driving your car with the emergency brake on. It would be extremely hard to drive that way, wouldn't it? Now imagine going about your life, not realizing you're driving with your mental emergency brake on. The majority of the population lives in exactly this way. For most people, the best way to start moving forward in life is not by pressing harder on the gas pedal, but to *release the brakes*.

All of God's commandments are summed up in this one phrase: Love God and love others as yourself. The Lord's heart is overjoyed when He sees your tender heart toward others. The simple act of forgiving others and asking for forgiveness breaks down the walls between God and you and hyperspeeds your relationship with Him.

RELEASING THE BITTERNESS BRAKE

When you are separated from God, from others and from yourself, fear results, as well as anger with its many faces—resentment, bitterness, condemnation of others and/or self, etc.

Recall again how Jesus says that the summary of all the Old Testament laws is to love God and love people. In fact, the phrase "Love your neighbor as yourself" is found in eight different places in the New Testament. To Him, this is it—the greatest priority.

The opposite of loving others is to be angry and bitter toward them. This separation is Satan's objective, since he knows this is contrary to the deepest desire of his enemy, God. In combination, anger and unforgiveness make up the ultimate act of rebellion.

Anger and unforgiveness make up the ultimate act of rebellion.

So how are you to live in freedom from bitterness? When everything inside of you desires to be angry at that one person, you're probably asking yourself, "Why should I forgive?"

BECAUSE HE FORGAVE YOU FIRST

Once upon a time, there was a great king.

One day, the great king was going through his records and noticed that one of his servants, Larry, owed him $2.5 billion dollars. Sadly, Larry, who worked as a farmer, could not pay off this incredible amount with his meager income. So the king ordered Larry, his entire family and all that he owned to be sold in order to pay off the debt.

Larry came to the king, fell on his face sobbing and fervently begged the king to give him a chance to pay it back. Surprisingly and mercifully, he chose to cancel Larry's entire debt, just like that! No negotiations or questions asked. Larry went home feeling like he'd just won the lottery.

The next day when Larry was out celebrating his newfound financial freedom, he noticed another of the king's servants. It was Johnny, who still owed Larry $5,000. Larry sneaked up behind Johnny and immediately put him in a chokehold. "Pay me back my money!" he yelled.

When Larry released him from the chokehold, Johnny fell to his knees and begged for another week before paying back his debt. But Larry answered, "Pay up right now, or I'm sending you to jail!" Johnny didn't have the money, so he was tossed into the slammer until his debt was paid.

News of this story spread and eventually came to the attention of the king. Upon hearing what had happened, the king called Larry to his palace and reprimanded him:

> "You wicked servant! I forgave you all that debt because you
> begged me. Should you not also have had compassion on your
> fellow servant, just as I had pity on you?" And his master was
> angry, and delivered him to the *torturers* until he should pay all
> that was due to him. So my heavenly Father also will do to you if
> each of you, from his heart, does not forgive his brother his tres-
> passes. (Matthew 18:32-35)

God compares forgiveness to a financial transaction. To forgive is to legally cancel a debt. When you forgive someone, you make a commitment not to demand repayment of past debts. It is only in the context of your own forgiveness that you find the strength to forgive others. Otherwise, it's virtually impossible.

> Forgive as the Lord forgave you. (Colossians 3:13)

Imagine yourself sitting as a defendant in the heavenly court before the Judge of the universe. You hear him read the list of every offense you've committed during your entire life: deceit, lust, judging, gossip, slander, anger, self-righteousness, pride and much more.

After that most humiliating experience, you spend what seems like hours anxiously awaiting the verdict. Imagine hearing the angry tone of His voice as He declares you *guilty as charged*, and pronounces that you deserve

His full wrath for the horrific crimes you've committed against Him. Your sentence: eternal confinement and torture in the lake of fire.

You turn to the gigantic angelic bouncer next to you and say, "But, that's too much! Why do I deserve such a terrible punishment?!"

He answers, "One's punishment is always equal to the crime. You never understood how truly offensive you were to the One who gave you life. If you did, you would never even consider complaining about the severity of hell. The greater the crime, the greater the punishment."

You begin to imagine what it's going to be like to spend eternity in a very hot, dark place, thick with terror, despair and hopelessness. You have absolutely no hope of getting out of this pit. Zero. You'll hear men and women screaming in agony. You'll be subjected to the physical pain of unquenchable heat and the disgusting smell of sulfur and flesh that never stops burning.

You say to yourself, "What have I done?" The truth is, this is what you and I deserve. God is so offended by man's rebellion that He declared a death sentence on everyone.

But thank God, He's also a merciful Dad! His plan was to penetrate through the dimensional gap between Himself and mankind *on our behalf* to personally serve the death sentence we deserved. The Good News is that if you receive His gift of salvation *and* offer your life to Him, you will experience the most loving and astonishing tradeoff known to mankind.

> And he died for all, that those who live should no longer live for themselves but for him who died for them and was raised again.
> (2 Corinthians 5:15)

What happens when you choose to live a life of bitterness rather than one of forgiveness?

WHO IS THE TORTURER?

The Greek word for Tormentor is *basanistes*. Depending on which translation is used, it is translated tormentor, torturer or jailer. It is used only once in the entire New Testament. The literal meaning of the word tormentor is "one who elicits the truth by the use of the rack." This is a form of tying up a person to inflict pain by stripping off their skin.

It is clear that the tormentor is an evil spirit—whose job is to imprison and torture.

> But one whom you forgive anything, I forgive also; for indeed what I have forgiven, if I have forgiven anything, I did it for your sakes in the presence of Christ, so that no advantage would be taken of us by Satan, for we are not ignorant of his schemes. (2 Corinthians 2:10-11)

> "In your anger do not sin": Do not let the sun go down while you are still angry, and do not give the devil a foothold. (Ephesians 4:26-27)

> Hand this man over to Satan, so that the sinful nature may be destroyed and his spirit saved on the day of the Lord. (1 Corinthians 5:5)

To torment means, "to inflict great physical pain or mental and emotional anguish." How often have you prayed for relief from spiritual oppression, not realizing that the demon probably has to say, "I have every right to be here. Remember Matthew 18:34-35? The Great King sends me here. I have a personal invitation from you because of your bitterness!" And the only way to be liberated from this kind of torment is to forgive *from your heart* (Matthew 18:35).

MIND-BODY CONNECTION

Hundreds of research studies have shown that anger negatively impacts your physical health. There have been many medical books written about the connection between your thoughts and your body. Just consider these examples:

- When you get embarrassed, what happens to your face?
- When someone surprises you, what happens to your heartbeat?
- When you tell a lie, what happens with your blood pressure, sweat glands and pulse?
- When you're about to talk in front of a crowd, what's happens inside your body?
- When you're stressed, what happens to your neck and back muscles?
- When you're anxious about an upcoming test, what happens to your stomach?

Now, consider these biblical passages:

A cheerful heart is good medicine, but a crushed spirit dries up the bones... A heart at peace gives life to the body, but envy rots the bones. (Proverbs 17:22, 14:30)

Your emotions always trail behind your repeated thinking, and your body always follows your emotions. What goes on in your thinking affects the rest of your body. If even mild emotions have an impact, how much more will the power of anger and bitterness affect your body?

RESEARCH STUDIES ON BITTERNESS

There are hundreds of studies conclusively proving the negative effects of bitterness.

Professor Elmer Gates of the United States Government Laboratory in Washington D.C. has made some astonishing discoveries using double microscopes. One of these was that anger, worry and fears poison the bloodstream. During his experiments, a test subject's breath was passed through a tube cooled with ice, which produced a colorless liquid. When the participant became angry, the liquid always turned into a brownish liquid substance. When Gates injected this brown substance into the vein of a guinea pig, the guinea pig died within a matter of minutes.

Under a microscope, a healthy person's blood looks like a flowing river. An angry person's live blood culture is clumpy and murky. Dr. Patricia Felici, a clinical nutritionist, did a finger prick on six people to test their blood and observe live blood cells. In this instance, three of the six people tested had a murky blood culture. She tested those three once again five minutes after they had released their bitterness by forgiving, and she found that their blood was free flowing.

> *The hatred you're carrying is a live coal in your heart—far more damaging to yourself than to them.—Lawana Blackwell*

Studies at Tufts, Cornell, and Stanford University have shown that repressed anger kills millions of people a year by way of suppressing the immune system causing destructive illnesses including heart attacks, cancer and many more.

Anger and bitterness cause a tremendous amount of stress.

The Center for Disease Control estimates that ninety percent of all diseases are caused by stress. Dr. Bruce Lipton, a renowned cellular biologist from Stanford University Medical School and a *New York Times* best-selling author, states that ninety five percent of all illness is caused by stress. The National Institute for Occupational Safety and Health as well as the American Institute of Stress estimates that ninety five percent of doctor office visits are stress-related.

Remember that stress from anger and bitterness will always cause health problems. However, it's important to keep in mind that not all health problems are caused by stress. Some illness is related to environmental and nutritional influences, trauma, the use of medications, etc.

In general, the effects of these other influences would be either non-existent or at least kept to a minimum if your immune system was not so radically affected by deadly emotions. Your immune system has an amazing ability to heal itself when you are free from bitterness.

Physical healing from habitual anger is not something that generally happens overnight, and the results of the healing also tend to manifest themselves in a gradual fashion. It is very often the case that people desire to be healed far more than they desire reconciliation.

The following is the sequence of events that occurs when you become angry or bitter:

1. An evil spirit plants a lie in your mind—against God, others and yourself.
2. You meditate on the lie and believe it.
3. This results in angry and bitter feelings toward God, others and yourself.
4. Cortisol is released into your blood stream and slowly destroys your immune system, leaving you vulnerable to all sorts of illnesses.

Toxins are imprisoned in your body until you release yourself with the key to your own healing: forgiveness. When you start forgiving, the cells start releasing toxins. As a result, you experience an emotional and a physical detoxification.

When You Forgive

Since I've implemented the daily habit of forgiving others and myself, I have experienced significant healing. I've been healed of chronic fatigue syndrome, allergies, insomnia, neck and back problems, teeth grinding while sleeping, hypoglycemia, immune system deficiencies, acne and skin problems.

What's interesting is that I never even set out to get rid of these health issues. I wasn't even aware that bitterness or forgiveness actually affected my body! It felt so good to finally be released from the oppressive and destructive claws of these illnesses. Words can never describe how excited I am to wake up everyday with a heart and body that is full of forgiveness.

The truth is, the benefits of forgiveness don't stop with physical healing. I've read about businessmen who doubled their income within a few months of forgiving their parents. The fact is, releasing your anger enables you to have more focus and energy to better accomplish your job.

Jack Canfield, creator of *Chicken Soup for the Soul,* gives his audience an opportunity to deal with life regrets at every one of his speaking engagements. After twenty-plus years of speaking all over the world, the top two regrets he hears are these: (1) Not forgiving people, (2) Not sharing encouragement or taking the time to do a good deed for someone.

WHEN YOU DON'T FORGIVE

Fred is a successful stockbroker and is well respected at his firm. One day, while eating lunch with his co-workers, Fred went back to his desk to get something. Upon his return, he discovered that his friends had hidden his lunch. Fred exploded and began yelling, demanding that they return his lunch. Bill, the perpetrator, finally pulled Fred's lunch from the fridge and gave it back to him. By then, the tension in the room was unbearable.

After peace was restored, Bill, who was Fred's best friend, asked Fred a pointed question: "Why did you overreact in the lunch room? It was just meant in fun. What was the big deal?"

After taking some time to reflect, Fred answered, "When I was in junior high, there was a big bully who picked on me. He always either took my lunch money or stole my food."

"That had to be very frustrating," Bill said. "Have you ever forgiven him?"

Fred stared at the floor. His non-response was answer enough.

By then, Bill was beginning to understand Fred better. Desiring to understand him even further, he asked, "So why do you get so upset when the manager corrects you during our meetings?"

Fred responded candidly, "I guess I feel like he's talking to me the way my father did, always criticizing the mistakes I made. Bill then asked, "Have you forgiven your dad?" Fred quickly replies "Never! I still can't stand that about my dad. He's always critical." Fred had never forgiven his junior high nemesis or his father's shortcomings. Because of that, he tended to overreact in the here and now. It made him unteachable and irritable.

If you struggle with closed-mindedness, it's probably because you have never taken the necessary steps to forgive your parents and other authority figures. When anyone talks to you with the slightest tone of correction—anything that hints of authority—you'll probably overreact. You're not reacting to the person presently talking to you, but to your dad or the authority in your past that you feel has offended you.

Unforgiveness cannot be stuffed down without revealing itself later. It's like dynamite waiting to be ignited by any situation that reminds you of the past. Behind every ugly family split, divorce, or lost friendship is an unforgiving heart.

Overreactions are rooted in the soil of unforgiveness.

When it all boils down to it, you struggle with unforgiveness because deep down you have a broken heart. The more unforgiving and angry you are, the more hurt you have buried deep inside. In the end, you need to share your hurts to your heavenly Dad, and ask Him to help you interpret your past through the lens of faith. He's understanding and compassionate to those with broken hearts.

> The LORD is close to the brokenhearted and saves those who are crushed in spirit… He heals the brokenhearted and binds up their wounds. (Psalm 34:18; 147:3)

ACTION POINTS

I encourage you to find a friend, a brother or sister, or your small group to team up with in establishing and reinforcing the habits you learn in this book.

1. Ask for Forgiveness

As Kristy and I started learning about the blessings of forgiveness, the Holy Spirit spoke into our hearts, encouraging us to contact people who we had wronged in the past. Some of the issues I rationalized as trivial, yet they had been haunting me for a very long time. We decided to contact everyone who came to mind, no matter how small or great the offense.

We hadn't talked to some of them for a long time. I dreaded talking to them! I felt ashamed and definitely humbled. What if they got mad at me? What if they blew up at me? I was mortified to make contact with these people. Though I struggled with this task, I knew that this was something we had to do.

To our surprise, most people were happier to hear from us than they were upset about the situation that we were asking forgiveness about. They were very impressed that we have would even ask for forgiveness for the offenses that we brought up. Some were inspired to do the same thing and ask forgiveness with people that they have offended.

After we had finished, we both felt as if tremendous weight had lifted off our hearts, a weight we didn't even realize was there! I couldn't believe how much better I felt. I was surprised at how much easier the process was than I anticipated.

I realize that not everyone will experience the positive outcome Kristy and I did. There may be tears and unforgiveness from those you contact. In truth, you may face total rejection, but still you must ask forgiveness, for your sake. You must humble yourself and listen to their side of it without defending or attacking them in response, especially when the other party has been guilty of wronging you and is not apologetic.

Here are points to keep in mind when you ask for forgiveness:

- *Take responsibility*—Confess the action or words that offended or hurt them without blaming, justifying, or attacking. "I'm sorry for calling you a jerk in front of everyone." "I'm sorry I left you when you needed me the most."
- *Talk about the consequences*—To the best of your ability, confess what your actions or words have cost them. "I realize that I disrespected you and humiliated you in front of your employees and possibly damaged your reputation."
- *Connect with them*—Share with them the godly sorrow you feel over your behavior. "I feel terrible for doing that. I can only imagine how much it hurt you."
- *Ask for forgiveness*—At the end of the conversation, ask them to forgive you. "In spite of what I've done, would you please forgive me?"

- *Make it right*—If you owe something, make it right. "Is there any-thing I can do to make it right with you?"

Now pick up your pen. Close your eyes, take a deep breath and ask the Holy Spirit to bring to mind those whom you need to ask forgiveness from. I've already been praying for you long before you picked up this book.

NAMES	YOUR OFFENSE
_____	_____
_____	_____
_____	_____
_____	_____
_____	_____
_____	_____

DATE to call the people listed: _____

2. Forgiving Others

Since Kristy and I decided to make it right with those we wronged, we also went through the process of forgiving those who had offended us. The thing is, those who've hurt us in the past usually have to be forgiven again and again. I didn't realize that forgiveness involves forgiving on a daily basis. Believing forgiveness was a one-time event was one of the biggest lies I fell for.

When I notice that I'm having imaginary conversations with certain in-dividuals, I know it's time to forgive them *again*.

Kristy and I forgive each other daily in our marriage. We've noticed that every so often, we can have a tendency to be snippy or short with each other. Some of the irritations are so trivial that it's difficult to understand why we react the way we do. This is what we've learned:

Overreactions are rooted in the soil of unforgiveness.

Because of this, we implemented a new and most excellent habit in our marriage. Every evening, we ask each other this question: "Is there anything for which I need to ask forgiveness?" The one who needs forgiveness is not allowed to defend or rationalize in any way. He or she is just to validate and apologize. Since we've implemented this daily practice, we've noticed that the snippiness has lessened significantly.

When one of us overreacts, we make it a point to avoid over-analyzing that situation, with the awareness that other unforgiveness issues in the past could be causing the overreaction. Now, we go through a quick discovery process where we say, "I think I overreacted in this situation as a result of something you did or said earlier."

Dr. Frederick Diblasio of the University of Maryland, a family therapist who has had tremendous success with forgiveness, use the power of forgiveness to reconcile couples when every other attempt at reconciliation had failed before they came to him.

One of the best lessons I've learned about forgiveness came from a friend of mine. We were talking about an injustice that happened to his family, and I was really upset on his behalf. Finally, I asked how he could be so forgiving. He said, "As a general rule, people don't wake up in the morning planning to be monsters. Everyone just does the best they can at the time." And even though I didn't completely agree, I've adopted this mindset toward other people. In doing so, I've become more gracious and understanding toward others.

Forgiveness is the key that can unshackle us from a past
that will not rest in the grave of things over and done with.
As long as our minds are captive to the memory of having been wronged,
they are not free to wish for reconciliation with the one who wronged us.
—Lewis B. Smedes

Below is a guide to forgiving those who have wronged you. Remember to put yourself on top of the list. Now is also the time to release yourself from your failures, mistakes and self-condemnation. Your Father in heaven is near you; you're not going through this alone. I'm sorry for the pain and trauma you've had to endure, but now is the time to be set free.

Ask the Holy Spirit to bring to mind who it is you need to forgive. Remember that forgiveness is a process, a difficult and life-long journey, not a destination. Breathe deeply, and with your eyes closed, listen to your heart. Humble yourself before God, and I guarantee you, He'll show you exactly who to forgive.

NAMES   **THEIR OFFENSE**

_____   _____

_____   _____

_____   _____

_____   _____

_____   _____

_____   _____

1. Acknowledge the event and your emotional pain. One of the ways the human mind responds to trauma is to stuff it down and pretend it never happened. Denial is very unhealthy, for it will show up in unexpected places at inopportune times. Part of the difficulty with forgiving is to revisit the past and allow yourself to finally *feel* the pain of the injury and allow yourself to grieve—"I was hurt when…"

2. If you've been violated or abused in any way, realize that you're not a bad person. It's perfectly normal to be fearful and hurt after what

happened. For those of you who've been abused, please know that your rights have been violated. You were wronged, and it wasn't your fault. You are not to blame—"I was hurt by…"

3. Specify the words said or actions done and what it cost you—"All I wanted was…"

4. Forgiving someone may mean reconciliation, but because it takes two people to resolve an issue, there's no guarantee. There are certain individuals who won't respect you even with the boundaries you've set. I have prayed that God would bring healing and reconciliation with your relationships. "I understand…"

5. Release them from the obligation of paying you back for the debt and damage they have committed toward you—"I completely forgive and release you for…"

6. Realize that they are not their sin. In Romans 5–8 we learn that we need to differentiate people from their sin. Separate them from their sins in your heart.

7. Remember how much God has forgiven you—"Thank You, Lord Jesus, that You've forgiven me from…"

8. Drink lots of water. Toxins that have been stored in your body will be released. If the water isn't there to flush the toxins out, your immune system will be compromised.

9. Mentally picture the people or that person in front of you. Tell them these words: "I forgive you for what you've done and said. I love you not because you deserve it, but because my God first loved me. I completely release you for what you've done."

10. Pray for that person's well being. Besides praying, mentally plan on doing good to those you need to forgive: encourage them; give them money; serve them; etc.

TIME OF THE DAY to do your daily forgiving: _____

ACCOUNTABILITY PERSON to share this with: _____

Forgiveness is a journey. Forgiveness is not a one-time event but a lifestyle, a way of life. It's extremely important that you do a daily time of releasing those who have hurt you in the past. I'm absolutely ecstatic for what's going to happen with your life from this first habit!

Forgiveness is God's most powerful message to the world.

SUMMARY

1. Forgiveness releases the brakes and allows you to start moving forward.
2. Your heavenly Dad desires for you to forgive others since He first forgave you.
3. Anger and bitterness cause your body to warn you of danger in your heart.
4. Bitterness makes you irritable and unteachable.

DISCUSSION QUESTIONS

1. How often do you have imaginary conversations with those you're upset with?
2. Do you have tendencies to stuff down your anger towards others?
3. Is it hard for you to say, "I'm sorry," to those you've hurt?

PRAYER

Thank You, Lord, that You have released me of all my offenses, past, present and future. I'm overwhelmed with Your unconditional forgiveness. I release those who have hurt me. Help me make a daily habit of freeing myself so I'm able to deepen my relationship with You and others, since You took the initiative and loved me first.

CHAPTER 8

HABIT #2: RECEIVE

Opening Your Heart

*There's nothing worse than desiring something you don't
have, only to not receive it when it is given to you.*
—ANONYMOUS

Unless you have received, it is impossible to give.
—ANONYMOUS

The only way that you can take possession of a gift is by having the
ability to receive.

Receiving means, "to take in; to hold; to contain; to allow or to accept;
to believe."

After releasing the brakes of bitterness and implementing the daily
habit of forgiving with Habit one, the first step to moving forward is to learn
how to receive. This habit opens up your heart to all that God desires to
share, give and teach you.

What will life be like if you lived like this?

Blessed is the man who fears the LORD, who finds great delight in
his commands. Even in darkness light dawns for the upright, for
the gracious and compassionate and righteous man. Surely he will
never be shaken; a righteous man will be remembered forever. He
will have no fear of bad news; his heart is steadfast, trusting in the
LORD. His heart is secure, he will have no fear; in the end he will
look in triumph on his foes. (Psalm 112:1,4,6-8)

Does this guy sound like he ever struggles with stress, even through hard times? What if you could respond to difficulties and bad news like he does? Wouldn't that be a great way to live?

It's a reality anyone can have.

Why then, are so many Christians stressed, defeated, sick and tired? One of the main reasons is because in their hearts they've never truly believed and received the fact that God loves them. They've been taught the following basic premises that are actually half-truths:

1. Just learn the facts in the Bible.
2. Do good to gain society's approval as well as God's approval.
3. Eliminate unacceptable behaviors to prevent rejection by others.
4. God's approval is dependent on your ability to hustle and do better.
5. You're not that valuable, so don't receive any compliments or gifts.

In the end, all theological truths revolve around this verse:

For God so loved the world that he gave his one and only Son,
that whoever believes in him shall not perish but have eternal life.
(John 3:16)

It's essential for you as a believer to be able to receive from God. The ability to receive and experience God's love is the only remedy to the internal longing that says, "There's more to life than this." Many Christians struggle for that elusive something they can't even name—something they frantically chase.

You deeply long for something you can't describe, the stamp of approval that surpasses anything you've ever known. If you won't receive love from people whom you can see, how do you expect to receive unconditional love from a God that you can't see? The inability to receive all God's love and encouragement will, in the end, produce a mountain of stress.

The truth is, you can *give* only to the extent that you've received. You can only encourage others to the extent that you have *experienced* God's encouragement and approval. This principle is even contained in God's promise to us through our ancestor, Abraham:

I will bless you… and you will be a blessing. (Genesis 12:2)

Your friendship with God is the most life-altering *blessing* you could ever experience. God can change the world through you, once you grasp the depth of this truth.

He did through Abraham.

Think about this question: What would have happened if Abraham had refused God's blessing? What if he had rejected God's proposal because he felt he wasn't worthy, that he was just a worm? He had absolutely no idea what was at stake by receiving God's promises. Am I ever glad he received it!

More than anything, God wants to tell you, demonstrate to you and prove to you that He really does love you. He went *far beyond the call of duty* to communicate this message, stepping out of one dimension and into another. Once you join His family, you leave the stressful courtroom of heaven and step into His warm and welcoming family room!

Once you join His family, you leave the stressful courtroom of heaven and step into His warm and welcoming family room!

Your desperate need to be loved is quenched only by your ability to receive. Receiving is agreeing that God's opinion of your value and worth is true. Receiving is to your heart what eating is to your body. It's the key to growing and nourishing your heart. It's the door that opens up your heart to the much-needed water of approval you have thirsted for in the past and are starving for in the present.

A slow death eventually occurs when you don't eat. In the same way, your heart slowly dies, starving until it receives God's approval. You will ravenously look for this love in all the wrong places. As mentioned earlier, every addiction is rooted in the need to be loved. All sorts of emotional anesthetics and perfectionistic pursuits follow the heart that's never been loved.

Refusing to receive God's unconditional love is to call Him a liar, believing your own standard instead of God's. Have you ever noticed how difficult it is for most people to receive compliments? I once heard a speaker say that he discovered, after thirty years of being a psychologist, that over ninety percent of the general population have a hard time receiving a simple "Thank you." Most of us have been taught to try harder, do better and give more. We have not been taught to receive in a heartfelt and humble manner.

What happens to your life when you don't receive?

HUMILITY AT ALL COSTS

Sharon grew up with a dad who taught her to be humble.

Elmer, who pastored a large church in Nevada, taught his daughter that accepting praise or encouragement might make her conceited and prideful. Sharon was clearly taught how to *not* receive. Elmer never encouraged Sharon. Growing up, he neglected to praise her for any success she had as a kid. He never expressed that he loved her, was proud of her, or believed in her—all because he feared that Sharon might become prideful.

At a young age, Sharon struggled with self-condemnation and could not believe God liked her, let alone loved her. Though her dad never yelled at her or told her anything negative, his silence was like a knife slicing to the core of her heart. To this day, Sharon is frantically pursuing perfection, living the fantasy that if only she could be good enough, her dad would say he was proud of her, and she could finally feel the elusive approval of God.

Any time you compliment, encourage, or praise Sharon today, she gives you a blank stare. She struggles to receive approval in every area of her life. When offered money or acts of service, she politely turns them down. She emotionally escorts the giver out of the inconvenience of helping her, as if it would be an imposition.

Elmer didn't realize he could actually teach someone how to receive love—*with a humble spirit.* Just because there's a potential for pride doesn't mean it will actually happen. It is just a possibility, not a guarantee. It is not an excuse to forsake his responsibility to nurture and empower his daughter to become a lifetime overcomer. That's why it's crucial to provide sound biblical teaching and most of all, modeling, in regard to healthy receiving with humility.

Because this concept is so crucial, Kristy and I encourage every little success in our children as well as with each other. Though we compliment them for being cute, we spend the majority of the time encouraging their inner qualities—such as being loving and responsible in these formative years of their lives.

We also have a nightly routine with our kids where we sit down with them and say, "Look at my eyes. The beauty I see in you is...." We spend time telling them all that we appreciate about who they are. We remind them that we're proud of them, we believe in them and that we love them. Believe it or not, our four-year-old daughter actually does the same to us. What a beautiful way to end a night, with love and affirmation.

We choose to speak life to our children because we are their only example of God right now. It's important to realize that we as parents create either an environment where our children will receive God's love, or an environment where they'll feel unlovable, rejecting God when they grow older.

My Experience with Receiving

All through my growing up years, encouragement was something I hardly saw in society. I also found that because of the lack of modeling in this area, when I did receive compliments, I had difficulty accepting these expressions of love.

Over the years I've learned to receive acts of service and gifts, but I've always been uncomfortable hearing empowering words. When I heard personal encouraging words, I had no idea how to process them. I just knew that inside, I felt a weird emotion that I couldn't define. Later, I learned that this uncomfortable emotion stemmed from the conflicting feelings of gratitude and unworthiness.

When I left the ministry, I became involved with sales and marketing. Through the years I went to more and more sales training events so I could improve in my trade. Later as I started and ran my own business, I attended many success seminars. I met a lot of successful entrepreneurs during that time.

From my interactions with these entrepreneurs, I experienced about ten times more encouragement than I ever did in the "ministry world." Incredibly, I've felt accepted, valued and empowered by these people even through sharing with them my mistakes and struggles. I didn't think such a group of people existed in this world! It was a great context to learn how to receive, since receiving wasn't my expertise.

I long for the day where I see this kind of encouragement in the context of every local body of believers as well as in the global Church at large.

Do You Receive?

Jesus said, "Whoever believes in me, as the Scripture has said, streams of living water will flow *from within him*" (John 7:38). He did *not* say that this deep, abundant flow would come from whoever hustles the most and outperforms everyone.

Here's a quick quiz to help you know how strong your receiving muscle is. This is a Yes or No quiz. If your answer is somewhere in the middle, pick the answer that's most true to your heart.

1. Do you have difficulty receiving large sums of money as a gift? ____
2. Do you have difficulty being praised in front of a large group? ____
3. Is it hard for you to receive kind words without saying anything nice in return? ____
4. Do you divert the subject or minimize yourself when receiving compliments? ____
5. Do you find it hard to accept it when someone volunteers to help you with anything you're doing? ____
6. Do you have a hero mentality, preferring to give, help and serve others rather than being the recipient of a blessing? ____
7. Do you have difficulty believing and feeling that God unconditionally loves you, and that He's actually happy with you? ____
8. Do you feel uncomfortable when someone shares with you his or her heartfelt appreciation for your friendship? ____

How did you do with the test? Are you an excellent receiver, or do you struggle with being blessed?

SATAN'S PLOT TO KEEP YOU FROM RECEIVING

I can't stress enough that one of Satan's strategies is to create the misconception that he is a non-factor. If you think he's just in his family room watching ESPN, you are fatally mistaken. Satan knows that only your ability to receive can fill the void inside of you. To prevent this, he has come up with some twisted truths to keep you from being truly close to your heavenly Dad.

When you don't receive from God, you start to feel fear. Fear has been disguised today under the title *stress* and *anxiety*. Here are some of the most common fears and accompanying lies you face when you feel separated from God:

- *Poverty*—"God doesn't love me enough to provide for my needs."
- *Abandonment*—"God will leave me hanging sometime soon."
- *Pain and death*—"God isn't powerful enough to protect or strengthen me through this."
- *Rejection*—"God loves me, but He doesn't really like or approve of me."
- *Failure*—"I'll avoid being a failure at all costs, for failure equals rejection."
- *Change*—"My desire, more than anything, is to stay in my comfort zone. Change is scary."
- *Being controlled*—"I need to be in control; otherwise, someone will take advantage of me."

Unless you personally experience a supernatural relationship with God—*stress*—will rule the day. Here's an illustration that demonstrates the importance of receiving (Note that I use the term *receive* interchangeably with the word *believe*).

LESSONS ON DIRTY FEET

It was a chilly evening, as the cold penetrated the living room where Jesus had gathered for His last dinner with His twelve friends. They lit the braziers to stay warm. It was the annual Passover Feast. While dinner was still on their plates, Jesus got up from the table. He pulled off His outer garment, then wrapped a towel around His waist and tied it behind His back.

He walked around the outside perimeter of the U-shaped table, carrying a pitcher of water, a towel and a basin. The apostles all sat up, looking at each other with silent shock on their faces, giving each other a look that said, "Now what's He doing?" Without saying a word, Jesus knelt and removed the sandals of the disciple on the end, and began to wash his feet with water. Again, without saying a word, He removed the towel from His waist and dried the feet of His astonished follower, while preparing to move to the next man.

Just an hour earlier, the apostles had been arguing over which of them would be the greatest in the Kingdom. Now they sat in silent protest convinced they were not worthy of this honor. In their culture, no servant should ever have their master kneel before them, let alone wash their dirty feet!

When Jesus arrived in front of Peter, Peter defiantly pulled his feet back in refusal, looking around for social approval from the rest of the crew. He asked his Teacher, "Lord, are You going to wash my feet?" Jesus continued to reach for Peter's sandals, as if He had never heard Peter's protest. He responded, "You don't realize what I am doing now, but later you will understand."

Peter, who bravely and firmly retracted his feet further, said, "No, You shall never wash my feet." Without looking up, Jesus continued to gently reach for Peter's sandals, and responded, "Unless I wash you, you have no part with Me." This ultimatum didn't make sense to Peter at the time. While Jesus was finally washing Peter's feet, Peter asked, "Then Lord, not just my feet but my hands and my head as well!" Jesus, in His logical fashion, quickly responded, "A person who has had a bath needs only to wash his feet; his whole body is clean…"

When Jesus finished washing and drying the last disciple's feet, He stood, washed His own hands and went back to the head of the table. He reclined in His seat, looking at the brooding faces that waited for some sort of an explanation. Finally the Teacher spoke.

"Do you understand what I have done for you?" He asked them.
"You call me 'Teacher' and 'Lord,' and rightly so, for that is what I am. Now that I, your Lord and Teacher, have washed your feet,

you also should wash one another's feet. I have set you an example that you should do as I have done for you…. Now that you know these things, you will be blessed if you do them." (John 13:4-17)

Until they experienced and received what it was like to be loved and served, they could not have the power to love and serve others. In fact, their ability to receive changed the course of history.

KEYS TO SUCCESSFUL RECEIVING

In the context of your relationship with God, just as in everything else in life, there'll be a give-and-take aspect. I'm sure you've figured out already that He is the more giving and loving one. He absolutely delights in giving to His kids, and it just kills Him when you don't receive.

Belief and trust come from repetitive hearing and concentrated meditation on what He wrote to you in His Bible, with the assistance of the Holy Spirit. The more you get to know God, the more you'll grasp how much He unconditionally loves you.

Do not conform any longer to the pattern of this world, but be *transformed* by the *renewing* of your mind. (Romans 12:2)

The key to successful receiving is what I call "mental faith picturing." Let me explain each word:

- *Mental*—It's with your mind and heart/spirit (subconscious mind) that you know God.
- *Faith*—Belief or faith is a thought held as truth in your heart (subconscious mind).
- *Picturing*—It's been proven that the language of the heart is in the form of pictures.

Here are examples of how biblical figures used mental faith picturing in their minds:

All these people were still living by faith when they died. They did not receive the things promised; they only *saw them and welcomed them from a distance*. And they admitted that they were aliens and strangers on earth. People who say such things show that they are *looking* for a country of their own. If they had been *thinking* of the country they had left, they would have had opportunity to return. Instead, they were *longing* for a better country—a heavenly one. Therefore God is not ashamed to be called their God, for he has prepared a city for them. (Hebrews 11:13-16)

When she heard about Jesus, she came up behind him in the crowd and touched his cloak, because *she thought*, "If I just touch his clothes, I will be healed." (Mark 5:27-28)

These God-followers reasoned and pictured with their minds. By faith, they pictured a reality at a future distance that the human eye couldn't see. This is also the reason Jesus taught using word pictures:

On the last and greatest day of the Feast, Jesus stood and said in a loud voice, "If anyone is thirsty, let him come to me and drink. Whoever believes in me, as the Scripture has said, streams of living water will flow from within him." (John 7:37-38)

Listen! A farmer went out to sow his seed. (Mark 4:3)

Do you bring in a lamp to put it under a bowl or a bed? Instead don't you put it on its stand? (Mark 4:21)

For us today, the promise we hold onto is the fact that Jesus took the death sentence on our behalf. He loves and approves those who truly believe in Him.

THE PRACTICE OF MENTAL FAITH PICTURING

The conscious mind thinks in concrete facts and numbers. The subconscious mind thinks in pictures. Before you go to school, you mentally picture in your mind conversations you'll have. On the way to work, you picture the interactions you'll have.

Before any competition, competitors think about the outcome of the game. Those who usually do the best job picturing a win typically win the game. Of course, there are many other factors that come into play: experience, skills, age, strength, etc. All things being equal, the competitor who spends less time dwelling on losing typically ends up the winner.

Virtually all the top athletes in the world use this exercise. Mental picturing is when athletes not only picture their movements but imagine feeling them as well. In 1988, Canadian sport psychologists Terry Orlick and John Partington found that ninety nine percent of the 235 athletes they surveyed rely on this technique to prepare for a high-stakes race. Studies by the U.S. Olympic Training Center show that ninety four percent of coaches use mental rehearsal for training and competition.

I've heard Rick Warren say that no other habit can do more to change your life than daily reflection on Scripture. Harvard University researchers found that students who mentally pictured in advance performed their tasks with nearly 100 percent accuracy, whereas students who didn't achieved only fifty five percent accuracy.

The only difference with God's children is that what we picture in our hearts (subconscious mind) is not wishful thinking. It's based on the solid truths and promises of the Bible.

For centuries, God-followers have utilized the power of *mental faith picturing*. They mentally picture in their minds the reality of what the Scriptures say. Meditating on the Bible involves transferring your thoughts from the conscious to the subconscious—from your mind to your heart:

Do not let this Book of the Law depart from your mouth; mediate on it day and night, so that you may be careful to do everything written in it. Then you will be prosperous and successful. (Joshua 1:8)

Within your temple, O God, we meditate on your unfailing love. (Psalm 48:9)

I have more insight than all my teachers, for I meditate on your statutes. (Psalm 119:99)

You already do this exercise. I just came up with the fancy schmancy term *mental faith picturing* to help you remember this concept, and to differentiate it from something that most of us struggle with—mental *fear* picturing. Our mental pictures are often based on fear, bitterness, insecurity and so forth. The results are usually depression, anxiety, etc. Next time you talk to an anxious person, ask them what pictures usually come to their mind. With hardly any exception, they are fear-based pictures, rooted in lies.

Instead of mental *fear* picturing, why not picture in your mind these truths: God's unconditional love for you as His child; His forgiveness for all your mistakes—past, present and future; His relented wrath towards you because of what Jesus did; His customized and unique plan just for your life; His super powers to accomplish whatever He desires; and many more foundational truths about who God is and who you are in Christ.

When I started practicing *mental faith picturing* in my life, I noticed that my heart became a lot more thankful and much richer in praise than it used to be. Not only that, situations that would have been stressful, didn't seem all that difficult. It's bizarre because I feel like I traded my brain in for a new one. *Mental faith picturing* has absolutely changed my life!

WRONG PURPOSES

I also noticed that when I first started *mental faith picturing*, my motive for reading the Bible changed.

I'm sure you've already heard this advice: *Just read your Bible more*. And while that sounds good, most of the time I read it with the wrong purpose and motivation. I read it to work, to earn God's love and approval. After asking many people, I learned that I was in the majority with the rest of the church folks.

Reading the Bible with the purpose to earn God's love and approval interfered with my capacity to receive. My mindset—to work and to please—was based on the lie that I was earning God's approval, rather than trying to know God better. I read the Bible as a personal improvement blueprint. The idea of reading the Bible then became exhausting.

I again saw that my purpose always determines my stress level.

This is the reason I had a perpetual guilt feeling when I didn't read the Bible. Out of guilt, I pushed myself to read more, and when I was through, I vowed to "do better" next time. Now I read the Bible simply to know my heavenly Dad better, because He first loved me. I want to know Him in any and every way I can. I desire to live a supernatural life for His cause. The Bible has encouraging, life-giving words for me. It is my daily food. I can't live without it.

ACTION POINTS

Again, I encourage you to find a friend, a brother or sister, or a small group to implement the habits you learned in this section.

Your heavenly Dad wants you to live everyday receiving and believing that He really cares about you, and that He has everything perfectly under control. To this end, the following is a list of steps to help you strengthen your receiving muscle:

1. Receive from others

If you won't receive from people, chances are you'll have trouble receiving from the Lord, since "every good and perfect gift is from above" (James 1:17). When someone offers to give you something or to do something for you, or says something positive, you need to look them in the eye and say, "Thank you" with your whole heart and a sincere smile. This allows the blessing to penetrate deep into your heart.

Do not…
- offer them the option to back out, by saying, "You don't have to do that."
- rob them of the blessing of giving by saying, "No, thank you."
- minimize yourself in any way and convince the giver you don't deserve it.
- return the favor out of obligation.

2. Declare the truth

Kristy started this tradition in our family: Throughout the day, we say these words: *I believe You, Lord!*
- I receive and believe that You're the Great Provider.
- I receive and believe that Your goodness and mercy shall follow me all the days of my life.
- I receive and believe that You've deleted and forgiven all my mistakes.
- I receive and believe that You love and care about me.
- I receive and believe that You're my Protector.

3. Memorize the Word

Recite this passage before meals, in the shower, while driving, while waiting in line at the grocery store, etc:

> I pray that you, being rooted and established in love, may have
> power, together with all the saints, to grasp how wide and long
> and high and deep is the love of Christ, and to know this love
> that surpasses knowledge—that you may be filled to the measure
> of all the fullness of God. (Ephesians 3:17-19)

4. Mental faith picture it

When you read the Bible, picture in your mind what you're reading and personalize it, rather than just simply reading words. (You'll learn this in more detail with Habit three).

What would your life be like if you fully opened your heart to His love for you?

SUMMARY

1. Receiving opens your heart to all that God wants to share with you.
2. Don't just try harder to love, become a better receiver.
3. Satan's goal is to prevent you from receiving.
4. Unless you receive, you will be unable to truly give.
5. Mental Faith Picturing enables you to receive better.

DISCUSSION QUESTIONS

1. Do you have difficulty receiving?
2. What area of receiving do you struggle with the most?
3. How do you typically respond when someone gives to you?

PRAYER

Father, help me receive all that You have for me.
Teach me how to receive with all my mind, heart and soul.
I want to receive and believe what You've given me,
for I know this makes You happy. I also know that I can't
love others sincerely and with power unless I have completely
received Your love. Thank You for loving me!

CHAPTER 9

HABIT #3: MEET WITH GOD

Pressing the Gas Pedal

*There is not in the world a kind of life more sweet and
delightful than that of a continual conversation with God.*
—BROTHER LAWRENCE

*When you read God's Word, you must constantly be saying
to yourself, "It is talking to me, and about me."*
—SOREN KIERKEGAARD

Your friendship with God is your single most important relationship.
Nothing can compare with it. Which means the time you spend talking with and listening to God is the single most important activity you will ever do.

Even if you…
kill a giant,
part the Red Sea,
or walk on water…

…it's absolutely nothing compared to your relationship with God. He desires a relationship with you a billion times more than He wants your service. He knows that intimate friendship *with* Him will result in dynamic service *for* Him.

As we covered in chapter seven, forgiving is the first step in releasing the brakes of your life. It removes the separation between God, others and yourself. Receiving is the foundational habit that opens the door of your heart to receive any other truths coming your direction, including the remaining five habits. Now you're ready to step on the gas pedal to blast forward with your relationship with God. God desires to be your Dad and listen to all your joys and disappointments. He wants to share with you His thoughts and heart about everything:

> Cast all your anxiety on him because he cares for you. (1 Peter 5:7)

> The LORD confides in those who fear him; he makes his covenant known to them. (Psalm 25:14)

Though there are hundreds of benefits and reasons that result from spending time with God, let me give you some reasons that are rarely mentioned.

1. There Is No Third Option

Unfortunately, there's no middle ground in this world. There's no such thing as *your* option. Even Jesus, when talking to the religious folks, actually said they only do what they've heard from their "father, the father of lies." Jesus never said that it was just their interpretation of the Bible, or their personality:

> You do what you have heard from your father.... You are doing the things your own father does.... You belong to your father, the devil, and you want to carry out your father's desire.... When he lies, he speaks his native language, for he is a liar and the father of lies. (John 8:38,41,44)

Those who claim to live the "Christian life," but ignore God by never talking or listening to Him in His Word, are following the path of Satan. Some people actually think that living for themselves is a third option. For those who are struggling with whether they could trust God or not, the truth is—they are not "on the fence" because "on the fence" is not a third option.

In reality, there are only two options: living for God or for Satan.

Here's the biggest set of lies in the history of lies. Don't spend time with your God because...

- you have enough knowledge and wisdom to manage your life.

- you have enough energy and strength to conduct your life.
- you have enough skills, gifts and talents to be productive.
- everything else is more important, including ministry.

If these sound familiar, you've been conned—scammed. You've believed a lie. The intention behind the lie is hatred. I don't know about you, but I absolutely hate being lied to. Satan's number one job description is to keep you from spending time with God and His Word. This is what he did in the Garden of Eden, and he's still doing it today. When you do begin to read God's Word, Satan usually plants thoughts like these in your head:

- It's about time you're reading again (This is the self-condemnation Strategy).
- You have two things to do right now. It won't take that long (The enemy knows you thrive when pursuing the dopamine highs that come with checking off your next task).
- You know you don't really understand what you're reading (Mental laziness).
- You're too tired. Sleep is much more important (Sleep is the ultimate source of strength).
- You can always do it later today (The disease of procrastination).
- You should read this book to feel good about yourself and win God's approval today.
- Going to church is all you need. You don't need to be digging in the Bible.
- You're not a reader, and you already read the Bible yesterday, so you're good for today.

All of your thoughts come from one of three different sources: (1) your own mind, (2) fallen angels—evil spirits, demons, (3) the Holy Spirit. Satan is a deceiver (Revelation 12:9). He plants thoughts in your mind and makes you think they're your own. Each lie has this objective: to separate and divide you from God, others and yourself. Most of the time it's in the form of accusation against God or other people's intentions.

All of your thoughts come from one of three different sources.

Remember that the battleground is in your mind, and your sword—your only offensive weapon—is what your Dad says in His book, the Bible. Your greatest ally is the Holy Spirit. Not all of your thoughts are yours. Follow the principles from James 4:7-8 when these bad guys plant deceptive thoughts in your head:

1. "Resist the devil, and he will flee from you…" When you start having thoughts that you know are not yours, this is what you should say: "No, I don't want it, go away in Jesus name" (Jude 8-9).

2. "Come near to God…" Since every addictive tendency is rooted in the need to be loved, praise Him that you are completely full of His love, and that He passionately delights in you. The Lord inhabits the praises of His people (Psalm 22:3), and when He does, He doesn't share the company with His enemies.

How do you know if a lie has sneaked into your thinking? Listen to your emotions. Are you feeling guilty, angry, or fearful? Listen to your body. Are you feeling fatigued? Are you breathing more shallow than normal? Are your shoulders slightly raised? Is your stomach in knots? Watch your interactions with others. Are you irritable and crabby? Are you thinking of your menu of emotional anesthetics to alleviate your internal misery?

When you feel there's a dark cloud above you, you know you've been picturing fear/lie-based pictures in your heart. Once you uncover the lie, immediately resist and praise. If you are not resisting on a daily basis, chances are, you are stressed. You have believed the lie that all of your thoughts are yours. You are either resisting the bad guys or you're resisting God.

2. You Are a Sheep

Did you know the Bible compares you to farm animals? Because I grew up in the city, the whole sheep reference had no meaning to me. Growing up, I had seen, umm…well, zero sheep!

The Bible mentions the word sheep around 150 times. In case you don't know anything about sheep, this is not a flattering comparison. They're always getting lost. The truth is, sheep are naturally affectionate, defenseless and in constant need of management. Shepherds, those who manage sheep, protect their flock with a high wall surrounding them and a gatekeeper guards the opening. This protects the sheep from thieves and wolves. The shepherd's voice is so familiar that his flock recognizes him, even in darkness.

When a lamb repeatedly wanders off, the shepherd will break one of its legs, put a splint on it and bind it up. While it's healing, he will carry the lamb on his shoulders. Once the leg heals, the lamb, now familiar and intimate with the shepherd, will stay close to the shepherd the rest of its life and never stray again.

You are much more inadequate, incompetent and needy than you'll ever realize. You're entirely blind without His voice guiding you, unable to figure things out with the dullness of logic. If you ever think otherwise, you are buying into a compelling lie, and deceiving yourself.

Jesus said,

I am the gate for the sheep… whoever enters through me will be saved. He will come in and go out, and find pasture. The thief comes only to steal and kill and destroy; I have come that they may have life, and have it to the full. I am the good shepherd. The good shepherd lays down his life for the sheep. (John 10:7-11)

For you were like sheep going astray, but now you have returned to the Shepherd and Overseer of your souls. (1 Peter 2:25)

3. To Distinguish Truth from Lies

For years, I didn't realize that I was in a prison created in my own mind. I was in a continual state of stress, anger and anxiety as I desperately attempted to distinguish truth from lies. I had created this prison because I didn't fully listen to God's voice.

Stress, anxiety and insecurity reside in your heart if you have chosen to shut God's Word out of your daily life. You will not be able to decipher and decode all the thoughts and suggestions that come into your mind. You will agonize to know whether it's from God or evil spirits since you don't have God's regular dose of truth to guide you in your decisions.

> Be transformed by the renewing of your mind. Then you will be able to test and approve what God's will is—his good, pleasing and perfect will. (Romans 12:2)

> Your word is a lamp to my feet and a light for my path. (Psalm 119:105)

You don't realize that the loud internal siren driving you daily is your longing to be loved. You've gotten content with your life of stress. The series of God-replacements and addictive emotional anesthetics you've created are a daily routine you label the "American Dream."

In reality, it's a nightmare. A candy-coated nightmare engineered by the father of lies.

4. Supernatural Productivity

If you are not tithing ten percent of your income, I encourage you to do so. If you're already doing this, I applaud you. I'm sure you've already seen that your ninety percent is going further than your 100 percent ever did.

> Bring the best of the first fruits of your soil to the house of the LORD your God. (Exodus 23:19)

Did you know that the same principle applies with the first fruits of your time? If you gave ten percent of your daily time to the Lord, your other ninety percent would go much further. Dropping your to-do lists and entrusting that time to the Lord is a leap of faith. Ten percent of a sixteen-hour day is approximately one and a half hours. Would you be willing to spend that time with God? Does that seem scary? It was for me.

There was a time in my life when I thought an hour with God was a gigantic stretch. The Lord since has shown me the supernatural benefits of this precious time. Now, on any given morning, I spend from one-and-a-half to three hours with the Lord. It's unbelievable how much energy, wisdom and productivity I have for the rest of my day. I am addicted to His presence. My time with Him was the foundation that set my mind for the following thirteen to fifteen hours I was awake.

I noticed something interesting after I engaged in this practice. Prior to giving God ten percent of my time, I would typically wake up in the morning consumed with anxiety over my to-do lists. Life seemed to stress me out from the time I wake up. I've made such a lifestyle out of stress that I wasn't even aware of my frantic-panic mentality, until I came face to face with peace.

When we first started this habit, we experienced greater resistance from the forces of darkness than we ever imagined. It was the most extreme oppression we'd ever felt. No wonder, spending time with God is the single most important activity we would ever engage in. The Lord will test your heart whether you would actually seek after Him (Deuteronomy 8:2, 16, Judges 2:22, Isaiah 48:10). At first, I didn't know what to do with this oppression I felt. Eventually, I learned to resist and praise, and discovered that my God is testing me to draw me closer.

Aside from these four compelling reasons to spend time with your Dad, ultimately, the most compelling one is the fact that you'll truly like Him when you get to know Him! Not to mention that He is the cool, satisfying, living water that you have thirsting for all your life.

The following Action Points are suggestions for your daily date with your Dad. At first, I carefully followed the outline. After a few months, I began to hear the guiding of the Holy Spirit, as He told me which parts I should focus on. Large volume of God's Word is the raw ingredient that the Holy Spirit uses to talk to you. Without it, most people interpret their wishful thinking as guidance from God. I've lost track how many times the Holy Spirit told Kristy and me individually to read a passage separately, only to discover later that the Spirit told us to read the exact same passage!

ACTION POINTS

Remember to find others to help you implement the habits you've learned.

1. Say Your Sorry

Just like you would in any other relationship. It's mandatory to admit and apologize for every way that you have offended God—the all knowing, all present, all powerful God (1 John 1:9). At the same time, remember that there is no condemnation for those who are part of His family (Romans 8:1). Here is a sample of how I restore my relationship with God: "My Lord, I'm really sorry for offending you when I did/said _____. Please give me the strength not to do that again. Thank You so very much that I am forgiven already for all that I have and ever will do."

2. Praise and Thank Him

I daily celebrate God's forgiveness and unconditional love. Praise and thankfulness is by far the best way to practice the art of receiving. I do this for about twenty to forty minutes, first thing in the morning. It completely softens my hearts for the rest of my time with the Lord. Many studies have shown that the first fifteen to thirty minutes of the day is when your heart is most open to suggestion and change. What better way to use this time than to worship and thank Him!

> Enter his gates with thanksgiving and his courts with praise; give thanks to him and praise his name. (Psalm 100:4)

3. Surrender to Him

I daily present myself to Him since He first loved me. I plead with Him to help me know Him better. I tell Him I want to see and hear Him today in whatever way He desires. I confess that I am blind and lost without him. I declare that I am open to do anything He desires for me to do.

Then Jesus said to his disciples, "If anyone would come after me, he must deny himself and take up his cross and follow me." (Matthew 16:24)

4. Share Your Heart

I believe this is the most neglected habit by a wide margin. I've noticed that one of the biggest obstacles in having a meeting with God and listening to Him occurs when I have heaviness in my heart. When you have issues in your heart, you end up reading a half-page of Scripture, only to realize you didn't get anything out of it. Sound familiar? It's critical that you come before God just as you are, not trying to impress Him. You must be as real as you can before Him, sharing all your thoughts and feelings.

Trust in him at all times, O people; pour out your hearts to him, for God is our refuge. (Psalm 62:8)

Cast all your anxiety on him because he cares for you. (1 Peter 5:7)

What you have to unload is usually a form of fear (anxiety, confusion, frustration over situations, etc.) and bitterness (hurts, offenses, disappointments, anger) that has clogged your heart and emotional arteries.

Kristy and I either do this practice together, or through journaling separately. We both journal in our laptops, we call it G-mailing our Lord. One time, I journalled for about ten hours. After I unloaded everything inside of me, I found myself praying for everything and everybody I could think of. When I was done, I couldn't believe how light my heart was, and how much energy I had for the next week! It was like drinking thirty shots of espresso.

Journaling is widely used in the medical community due to its uncanny ability to heal the sick. James Pennebaker, a University of Texas psychologist, discovered that regular journaling strengthens immune cells. Pennebaker says that sharing your feelings by journaling helps lessen stressful feelings, reducing the impact of these stressors on the body.

This habit worked great for David (See the Psalms).

I suggest that you journal between fifteen and sixty minutes a day. I heard once from Bill Hybel that besides reading the Bible, journaling is the one daily exercise he will not give up.

Other benefits of journaling:

- to clarify confusing thoughts and feelings
- to know yourself better
- to release the intensity of stressful feelings
- to track patterns and growth over time
- to improve your communication skills

God has designed you with the need to unload the heaviness in your heart. I have noticed, though, that the things I was planning to vent to the Lord end up minimized after I've spent time in worship. Worship has an interesting way of making my God much bigger than my problems.

God has designed you with the need to unload the heaviness in your heart.

5. Pray for Your To-Do-List

I daily humble myself and pray through each and every one of my to-do list items and personal meetings for the day. It ends up being a board meeting with my Lord, where He begins to dictate my to-do list. I also receive certain messages that I'm supposed to share with those I was planning to meet with during the day. I have found tremendous benefits in doing this, noticing that I am much more calm and relaxed throughout the day.

> You may say to yourself, "My power and the strength of my hands have produced this wealth for me." But remember the Lord your God, for it is he who gives you the ability to produce wealth, and so confirms his covenant, which he swore to your forefathers, as it is today. (Deuteronomy 8:17-18)

> Trust in the Lord with all your heart and lean not on your own understanding; in all your ways acknowledge him, and he will make your paths straight. (Proverbs 3:5-6)

Did you know that God has His own to-do-list for you? Why not meet with the smartest and most powerful Source in the universe? He is the ultimate parent, businessman, doctor, accountant, counselor, teacher and friend. Did you know that He could help you work much faster and smarter? Believe it or not, He's a much better informant than Google.

As an ambassador of God, here are things I pray for daily:

- pre-arranged miracles and anointing from the Holy Spirit (John 14:12)
- supernatural wisdom and understanding (Proverbs 4:7)
- a spirit of excellence (Proverbs 22:29)
- courage and faith to move forward (1 Chronicles 28:20)
- preferential favor before men (Daniel 1:9)

6. Battle for others

I once heard from David Cho, pastor of the largest church on the planet, that if he had another church to start, he would shut himself up in a room for three weeks and do nothing but pray.

If you remain in me and my words remain in you, ask *whatever* you wish, and it will given you. (John 15:7)

If you were in a close, loving friendship with God, you would never ask for anything offensive to Him. You would only want the things that make Him happy. Oftentimes, your fear of disappointment keeps you from dreaming. Isn't it better to have a hundred dreams with only fifty coming true, than to have only two fulfilled dreams with no disappointments? I heard one of our pastors share that he even prays for his good friends to move into his neighborhood, just because he likes being around them. You know what? They did!

7. Study the Bible

Once I have humbled my heart with praise and unloaded my heart of any heaviness, I am now ready to receive from Him. First, I read with the premise that He passionately loves me and desires to share His thoughts and feelings with me. I don't read for His approval.

When you miss your time reading, don't condemn yourself; just ask the Holy Spirit to show you the lie that you believed (if that applies), and start over. Every day is a new day! If you have thoughts that are jumping around your mind distracting you, don't fight them and keep reading—share them with Him. These are usually fears or areas of bitterness that have never been vented to God.

Here are a few suggestions for those just beginning to read the Bible. First, determine what time and place works best for you. Practice mental faith picturing. Read from your heart, not just to gain facts. Most of all, invite the powerful presence of the Holy Spirit.

If you have never implemented Bible reading in your daily routine, here is a suggested list to get you started:

- *A daily chapter from Proverbs*—There are thirty-one chapters in the book of Proverbs to correspond with the days of the month. If it's July tenth, read the tenth chapter. I also encourage you to find one verse in that chapter that hits home in your heart. Meditate on that verse, and memorize it for the day. *A chapter of Proverbs a day keeps the foolishness away.*

- *Psalms*—Make it a goal to read through five Psalms at night before going to bed. This ends your day with praise and worship.

- *The One Year Bible*—I know of many people who have been really encouraged by this type of Bible-reading schedule.

- *Relationships*—Try to read the Bible from cover to cover. Since your ultimate purpose involves relationships, have an eye specifically on the relational dynamics between God and people, people and people and people with themselves. I have found that talking to the Lord as I am reading really helps me to take to heart what I read.

- *Gospels*—(Matthew, Mark, Luke, John) The gospels are a good place to read if you haven't been in the habit of reading the Bible. It helps you get to know our Lord Jesus.

There are many books out there that teach you how to study the Bible so you can get to know God better. One that I highly recommend is *Living By the Book* by Howard Hendricks. For years I have benefited from his method of studying the Bible.

8. Mental Faith Picture it

The Bible mentions the word meditating twenty-four times. When you read His Book, make it a habit to mentally picture the stories you're reading and how the principles apply to you personally. When you do, the Holy Spirit helps you personalize the message of the passage.

Within your temple, O God, we meditate on your unfailing love. (Psalm 48:9)

> Reading the Bible without meditating on it is like trying to eat without swallowing.—*Anonymous*

Mental faith picturing helps you make observations on a passage that you would have never noticed if you were just reading. This helps you to deeply get to know and understand your Dad much better. Meditation helps the truth of His Word be tattooed in your heart.

9. Take a Rest Day

I once heard a pastor talk about taking one day off to do nothing but spend time with the Lord. He shared that he noticed that the other six days went further when he dedicated this one day to the Lord. I thought it was a great idea. Except it took me eight months to actually implement it. I had no idea how much I ruled my time! When I finally got around to it, I did notice how much further the other six days went and how much more productive I was.

If you keep your feet from breaking the Sabbath and from doing as you please on my holy day, if you call the Sabbath a delight

119

and the Lord's holy day honorable, and if you honor it by not going your own way and not doing as you please or speaking idle words, then you will find your joy in the Lord, and I will cause you to ride on the heights of the land and to feast on the inheritance of your father Jacob. (Isaiah 58:13-14)

Our God is a purposeful and wise God. He knew we needed rest for our minds, our hearts and our bodies once a week. This is why *He* set an example for us and did it first. This rest day could be done any day of the week. The purpose for this day was for our benefit (Mark 2:27).

On this day, we usually don't do any chores, remodeling, or any work related to employment. It's an extended time where we read, worship, journal, fellowship and just rest our bodies. On rare occasions we might busy ourselves during our designated rest day. But when we do, the rest of our week seems much more stressful, chaotic and exhausting. Since Kristy and I implemented this habit out of desperation, we have compiled stories upon stories of miracles that have occurred in our lives, daily! We included these habits in our lives out of desperation, not because we're super spiritual. Once we began to experience the blessing of spending time with Him, we can never look back and live the life of stress we once lived.

Your time with God is the single most important activity you'll ever do. Even preaching in front of 300,000 people in an enormous stadium is nothing compared to the importance of this single activity. I have prayed on your behalf that you will personalize this truth. Once you experience what it's like to soar on wings like eagles, you'll never want to go back to living in the dark despairing cave of stress.

SUMMARY

1. Meeting with God is the single most important activity you'll ever engage in.
2. Your thoughts come from three different sources. You need to learn how to resist the devil and draw near to God by praising Him.

3. Meet with God because: There is no third option; you're a sheep; it's the only way to distinguish truth; supernatural productivity.

DISCUSSION QUESTIONS

1. Do you meet with God daily? Why or why not?
2. What is your purpose for reading the Bible?
3. What lie do you believe that keeps you from reading the Bible?

PRAYER

Lord, I humble myself before You, realizing that I barely know what it's like to get to know You better. May Your Spirit teach me to become more intimate with You. Open my eyes to see the lies I've believed in the past regarding time spent with You. Help me to get comfortable sharing my heart with You. Thank You for always pursuing my friendship!

CHAPTER 10

HABIT #4: PRAISE AND THANK GOD

Counting Your Blessings

Gratitude unlocks the fullness of life. It turns what we have into enough, and more. It turns denial into acceptance, chaos to order, confusion to clarity. It can turn a meal into a feast, a house into a home, a stranger into a friend. Gratitude makes sense of our past, brings peace for today, and creates a vision for tomorrow.
—MELODY BEATTIE

Worship is the correct response to the presence of God.
—DOUG HANLEY

Your heavenly Father absolutely loves grateful children. I, on the other hand, grew up criticizing and complaining about everything. In my mind, I always thought about how things should be, and I excused this tendency because I considered myself to be a great and mighty visionary. As a result, I was often discontent and irritated with life in general.

I then saw a monumental movie called *Life is Beautiful.* This movie changed my view on how I should live the rest of my life. The story is about a father and son who were imprisoned by the Nazis during the war. The dad made a point to always be looking for the fun and good in every situation and maintained an attitude of gratitude. Joy was his shadow—so much so that his son never even knew they were imprisoned!

This story gave me a glimpse on how the abundant life was meant to be lived out.

Shortly after I watched this movie, Kristy and I went to an experiential adventure camp. Even though it was the most fun we've ever had, we endured the most grueling physical activities we've ever attempted.

We were encouraged not to complain about anything. I had absolutely no idea how difficult it was not to complain about physical pain and discomfort, sleepiness, hunger, imperfections from management and weird campers. It was the most therapeutic experience not to complain! I was completely changed. This one camp alone virtually eliminated my tendency to complain.

WHY WE COMPLAIN

Any two guys could be experiencing the exact same situation. One guy chooses to daily complain of all the thirty things that went wrong, while the other guy thanks God for a hundred daily blessings. One man lives a long healthy life while health issues due to anger and anxiety haunt the other. The difference is in the way they manage their thoughts and heart.

One man chooses to receive and celebrate God's love and approval. The other man chooses to attain and maintain God's love and approval through performance-based perfectionism. As a perfectionist, his goal is to find and eliminate imperfections, mistakes and failures in his own life. Two different men with two different purposes.

Since he's made such a habit of faultfinding in his own life, he can't help but be the same way towards others. This causes him to complain and criticize everyone and everything around him. Gratitude is a farfetched reality for him.

Your ultimate purpose will always determine whether you will be a person who find faults, or a person who finds the good and gives thanks in all situations.

Satan is the master accuser and counterfeiter. His goal is for you to accuse God, others, yourself and your circumstances, rather than living a life of gratitude and praise.

Do these responses sound familiar?

- griping about how you were badly mistreated in customer service situations
- complaining to everyone about the slightest physical discomforts you're feeling
- grumbling about the ways you've been wronged in both your past and present relationships
- nitpicking about everyone at the social gathering you just left
- whining about how your current situation is so terrible
- finding every last inaccuracy and personality defect in preachers and writers

Slander, gossip, complaining and discontentment have become the norm in our culture, even within Christian circles. I just didn't grasp the depth of the problem until God opened my eyes to see how my seemingly "soft" words were slandering.

> *When life gives you lemons, make lemonade and then sell it to all of those who get thirsty from complaining.—Napoleon Hill*

COMPLAINING IS CONTAGIOUS

Did you know that complaining is contagious?

I once heard someone make a complaint about a customer service issue at a particular retail store. I remember being impressed with his keen observation. But as a result, every time I was in the same situation as that man, I found myself annoyed with the same lack of service.

I wish he had never told me of his observation.

It saddens me to share this, but at one time I did the same thing with Kristy and infected her with my complaining and criticizing tendencies. She has the natural tendency to see the best in every situation and every person.

For the first seven years of our marriage, I corrupted her with my "keen insights" on how life could and should have been.

> Do everything without complaining or arguing.
> (Philippians 2:14)

> These men are grumblers and faultfinders... they boast about themselves. (Jude 16)

> And do not grumble, as some of them did—and were killed by the destroying angel. (1 Corinthians 10:10)

> He who conceals his hatred has lying lips, and whoever spreads slander is a fool. (Proverbs 10:18)

I've noticed that complaining and criticizing have disappeared since I began the habit of praise! This is an example of the *replacement principle* (repentance) at work. I can't thank the Lord enough for teaching me such a monumental concept!

LAW OF GRATITUDE

Gratitude and praise will absolutely revolutionize your life! You will like the new you when you implement the lifestyle of gratitude. I guarantee it.

The first exercise of gratitude Kristy and I learned is to wake up in the morning with praise. In our home, it's the first and most important part of our time with the Lord. Implementing this habit was difficult at first, but we forced ourselves, believing it would transform our lives. It did! Nothing brings the anointed presence of the Lord more than worship!

> In everything give thanks; for this is God's will for you in Christ Jesus. (1 Thessalonians 5:18)

We also end the day in praise and gratitude. Research studies have shown that whatever you read, see, listen to, talk about and experience during the last thirty minutes of the day has a huge influence on the quality of your sleep, which then impacts the next day. During the night, your subconscious mind replays and processes this late-night input up to six times more often than anything else you experienced during the day.

We've also chosen to carry on this habit with our children. Every night before they go to bed, we go through a process of thinking of five things that happened throughout the day for which to thank God.

At night, we do our best not to dwell on what we could have done better throughout the day. Those kinds of thoughts make us end up dwelling on failures, fears and frustrations. In the past when I used to let these negative thoughts stir in my mind, I struggled with severe insomnia. This lasted for many years.

> *If you concentrate on finding whatever is good in every situation,*
> *you will discover that your life will suddenly be filled with gratitude,*
> *a feeling that nurtures the soul.—Rabbi Harold Kushner*

Once we implemented this habit of gratitude and praise in our lives, we noticed a few changes:

1. Our minds began to look for the good in everything and everyone.

In the past, I always looked for what was wrong. Now, we look for things to praise God for in each social situation we attend. The times we do regress and go back to nitpicking, we gently encourage each other to look for the good. To be more accurate, *Kristy* encourages me to look for the good, since I'm the one more likely to slip back to the trap of complaining. When we do stay on course, we see more of the blessings in every situation, and we're also much more likely to learn from those we spend time with.

2. We have gotten to know our God better.

We've noticed that the more we thank and praise Him, the more we see blessings around us. The funny thing is, He's probably not blessing us more than He did before. It's just that we've chosen to open the eyes of our hearts to see His blessings in unexpected places. Gratitude is like a pair of magical glasses that illuminates the areas our mind was unable to see.

Up until this time, I had no idea God was so intensely involved in the smallest details of my life. This new mindset has also completely changed how I interpret my past!

> You intended to harm me, but God intended it for good to accomplish what is now being done, the saving of many lives. (Genesis 50:20)

3. We feel more loved than ever before.

Since we've heightened our hunt for blessings through gratitude, we began to notice that there is a divine conspiracy to shower us with as many blessings and miracles as possible. We feel like God's favor surrounds and follows in everything we do.

> Taste and see that the LORD is good... Surely goodness and love will follow me all the days of my life, and I will dwell in the house of the LORD forever. (Psalms 34:8; 23:6)

Gratitude has helped me from all the depression, sadness, anxiety, confusion and heaviness that I used to struggled with. In the past, when I felt distant from God, I didn't realize I had believed the lie that He was distant. My mind pictured Him standing silently behind a distant curtain of unavailability, frowning at my imperfections. But since I've started the habit of praise and gratitude, I've rarely had a day when I felt that He was "distant" from me.

Every day, first thing in the morning, I go through the foundational truths of the Bible and praise Him for each one. I praise Him for: coming to sacrifice His life on my behalf; forgiving all my wrongdoing; adopting me as His son; being super powerful; being capable to do anything; desiring to get to know me: being my ultimate provider; preparing a place for me in heaven; being one day closer to seeing Him; etc.

Going through this process on a daily basis has swelled my heart. I feel like I can conquer the world by the time I'm done thanking Him for these truths.

RESEARCH STUDIES ON GRATITUDE

Research studies on gratitude suggest that feelings of thankfulness have tremendous positive value in helping people cope with stress.

This comprehensive study is based on the research of Robert Emmons, psychologist and leading figure in the field of gratitude research based at the University of California, Davis, and by Dr. Matthew McCullough of Southern Methodist University.[2]

In an experiment with college students, those who regularly recorded their feelings in a "gratitude journal" were more optimistic, exercised more regularly and described themselves as happier than the control group of students who kept no journals but had the same levels of health, optimism and exercise when the experiment began.

> *When you are grateful, fear goes away and faith comes near.*
> *—Anonymous*

They also noted that those who kept "gratitude lists" over a two-month period were more likely to accomplish important personal goals than participants who did not keep a gratitude list. Subjects practicing this gratitude habit were also much more likely to help others with personal problems than the other control group subjects were.

If you're in the ministry, this is a must-have habit!

---

2. http://psychology.ucdavis.edu/labs/emmons

Adam Smith, in his book *Theory of Moral Sentiments,* concluded that people who choose not to embrace a lifestyle of gratitude cheat themselves out of happiness in life. The philosopher Cicero, born around a hundred years before Jesus, said that gratitude is not only the greatest of virtues, but also the parent of all others.

The truth is, what you think about will always expand.

So, if you would like…

- more enthusiasm and energy
- less stress and depression
- to reach out to others more
- to exercise more and have better health
- to achieve more of your goals
- to sleep better
- to feel more loved
- higher levels of positive emotions and life satisfaction
- more vitality and greater feelings of well being
- less struggle with envy and materialism
- more empathy and more generosity…[3]

…then all you have to do is praise your God more. You can make this change in your life!

Once I learned to praise God throughout the day, even on "bad days," it has transformed every other area of my life. It has become my secret access tunnel to the next dimension where God downloads His love to me and feeds my deepest longing for approval.

ACTION POINTS

Again, I encourage you to find a friend, a brother or sister, or your small group to implement the habits you learned in this section.

---

3. This list is the result of studies with hundreds of participants from Dr. Robert Emmon's book, *Thanks!: How the New Science of Gratitude Can Make You Happier.*

Praise and gratitude should be a part of your daily language. Praise Him...
- when you first get up in the morning and when you go to bed at night
- when your heart is heavy and confused
- when traffic flow is not accommodating you
- when someone offends or disrespects you
- when you're not feeling well physically
- when you're in the company of difficult people
- when you're dealing with an obstacle that seems impossible to deal with
- when you're dealing with a complex relational issue

Thank Him for...
- His extravagant and unconditional love
- the gift of God's Son, Jesus and the suffering He endured in your place
- the relationships He has blessed you with
- your situation, including your church, your home, clothing, a reliable car and good food

As your heart becomes thankful to God, you will start looking for little opportunities to express your deep gratitude to those who give to you in any way. This is an indirect way of thanking God. I guarantee that complaining and criticizing will disappear, and you'll never again want to return to a life of complaining, criticizing and slandering.

In the next chapter, you will learn the ways you can live out and express your experience with God—your relationship with yourself and with others.

Summary

1. One of the most powerful habits you can adopt is to thank God in all things.
2. Your purpose determines whether you will be a complainer or a thankful servant.

3. Complaining is a contagious disease.
4. According to numerous studies, a life of gratitude has life changing benefits.

DISCUSSION QUESTIONS

1. Deep inside, would you consider yourself a critical complainer?
2. What are the top ten things you are most thankful for in your life?
3. Do you have people to whom you need to give thanks to?

PRAYER

Dad, help me to know, understand and experience
Your gracious love for me. Teach me how to receive all the
love notes You send throughout the day. You know I desire to love
You more. Please guide me toward that end. May Your praise
be continually on my lips all the days of my life. Thank You, Lord!

CHAPTER II

AS YOU LOVE YOURSELF

The Way God Does

Love your neighbor as yourself.
—JESUS, MATTHEW 22:39.

*If you aren't good at loving yourself, you will have
a difficult time loving anyone, since you'll resent the
time and energy you give another person that
you aren't even giving to yourself.*
—BARBARA DE ANGELIS

God really likes you.

As the Creative Designer who constructed you, God desires for you to know, accept and celebrate who you are. He wants you to see yourself as He sees you. He wants you to accept and forgive yourself like He does. It brings Him great joy to know you're happy with the way He made you. He fearfully and wonderfully designed you. It is a direct insult to Him when you are down on who you are, or when you think higher of yourself than you should.

For you created my inmost being; you knit me together in my mother's womb. *I praise you because I am fearfully and wonderfully made;* your works are wonderful, I know that full well. My frame was not hidden from you when I was made in the secret place. When I was woven together in the depths of the earth, your eyes saw my unformed body. All the days ordained for me were written in your book before one of them came to be. (Psalm 139:13-16)

Now some of you might be hyperventilating from the phrase "love yourself." Let me explain what I don't mean. I'm not talking about unhealthy self-absorption, arrogance, or putting yourself before God and others. Your value of yourself is just another result, not the goal. The fact is, you already love yourself. *As yourself* (Matthew 22:39) is an assumed concept. The only question is *how* you should love yourself based on truth, not lies.

The problem is that most of us love ourselves in unhealthy manners. The way that we typically love ourselves is based on a lie—we believe we need to earn God's love through perfectionism. This misguided expectation leads to self-condemnation, stress, emotional anesthetics, and eventually, self-destruction. Not very loving, eh? The most loving thing you can do for yourself is to give your entire life to the most loving being—God. Denying yourself, as Jesus told us to do multiple times, is denying the path of lies that we use to quench the longing of our soul.

The main reason that most Christians get spooked out by the whole concept of "loving yourself," or even "talking to yourself," is because of their fear of being selfish and prideful—the fear of imperfection.

It is an indisputable fact that we all talk to ourselves. The only question is *how* you should talk to yourself. Here are a few of numerous examples of inner-talk in the Bible:

Why are you downcast, O my soul? Why so disturbed within me? Put your hope in God, for I will yet praise him, my Savior and my God. (Psalm 42:5-6)

Praise the LORD, O my soul, and forget not all his benefit–who forgives all your sins and heals all your diseases…(Psalm 103:2-3)

Be at rest once more, O my soul, for the LORD has been good
to you. (Psalm 116:7)

We see throughout the Psalms how David encouraged (which is a form
of loving) himself, *based on truth,* through difficult times, declaring God's
unfailing and great love over and over.

In contrast, Satan wants to separate you from yourself. To this end, he
wants you to think either way too highly of yourself (pride) or way too low of
yourself (self-hatred). He wants you to find foolish ways to take care of your
needs—*emotional anesthetics.* He wants you to be paralyzed by the fear of failure. He wants you to beat yourself up and condemn yourself for your mistakes
and failures. He wants you to learn facts in your mind, and never personalize
them in your heart. That's the picture of a disconnected individual.

If you've listened to the accuser and followed his lies, chances are, you
probably beat yourself up for your imperfections. You may have bought into
the lie that perfection is the goal. Perfection always uses the whip of self-condemnation as the motivation to obey, while a
love relationship uses gratitude and love as the
motivation for obedience (Romans 2:4).

> *By the time we've reached the
> age of eighteen, most of us have
> been told close to 150,000 times
> what we can't do.*

It's been said that by the time we've
reached the age of eighteen, most of us have
been told close to 150,000 times what we *can't*
do, and less than five times what we *can* do. With that in mind, is it any
wonder we don't do greater things than Jesus did?

The problem is that we've adopted the negative messages, believing
them to be true. Furthermore, we repeat those messages to ourselves on a
daily basis.

YOUR INNER-TALK

It's a typical Sunday morning at the Fourth Baptist Church of Smallville.
Sally sits on the sixth row back, thinking to herself...

I hope this message isn't gonna be boring today. I already know everything about tithing. I wonder where he got that tie—it's a little crooked. Didn't he look in the mirror this morning? Didn't his wife notice his tie was crooked? I guess some wives just don't care.

Hmmm, look at her dress. That is so cute. Gotta buy me one of those! I wonder where she bought it? What's her name by the way? I am so terrible with names. Uh oh, we have to pray now. I can't stand that my money situation has been so bad, now I have nothing to tithe today. I feel like such a bad Christian.

This guy next to me is probably wondering why I'm not putting anything in the offering basket. Maybe I'll roll up a dollar bill, so it looks like I'm at least putting something in. I'm never gonna pay my debt off. Wow, that was a long opening prayer. I wish that I could pray like that. Have I ever prayed longer than five minutes? My prayer life really stinks.

I wonder if I'm really a Christian. I'm such a failure when it comes to my quiet time. Well, Jesus has forgiven me from all my sins. I'm not going to guilt myself to death. Gotta get that dress, I wonder if I could find it online! But I have to lose another fifteen pounds to even wear it. I hate my body. Seems like no matter what I do, I just can't get rid of the last fifteen pounds. I need to work out more, but I'm so lazy. Guess I'm just getting old. Why couldn't I have her body?

I can't believe Randy didn't even look at me! I wonder if my hair looks funny today. I can't stand my hair! It never does what I want it to. I wonder if Randy's upset at me since I didn't call him back last Friday. Wow, I haven't called my mom in two weeks. I'm so disorganized. I hope the pastor forgets to make us "meet our neighbor." I hate that part of church...

This thought process for Sally happened in less than fifteen seconds.

Can you count how many negative things she said about herself? Did you know that according to leading psychologists, the average person talks to themselves around 50,000 times a day?[4] And about eighty percent of the time, that talk is negative. That's 40,000 negative thoughts about ourselves daily!

---

4. Joe Kolezynski, "Belief, Self Talk, and Performance Enhancement," *Selfhelp Magazine*, www.selfhelpmagazine.com/articles/sports/selftalk.html.

Here's another example of typical destructive inner-talk. You're driving to your friend's wedding. You notice that you're lost. You look all over your car for the invitation, but you can't find it. You decide to get off your cell phone to continue looking, to no avail. You immediately say, *You idiot! How could you forget the directions! Your sister is going to be so upset!* Talking to yourself in that manner has become such a habit that you don't even think twice about it.

It's very common that you've learned to talk to yourself in the same way your parents talked to you. Do you remember how they talked to you? Did you like it? Was it empowering and realistic, or was it belittling and sarcastic? Either way, have you considered that you may be imitating them with how you talk to yourself today?

It's a well-known fact that you'll come to believe whatever you repeat to yourself, regardless of the validity of the statement. If you repeat, "I can't sing," over and over, eventually you'll believe it as truth. Your beliefs are made up of repeated thoughts. Repetition is the key to long-term change. You are who you are today because of the contents of your repetitive thoughts, also known as your belief system.

With no exception, you will always live your life according to your beliefs.

THOUGHTS BECOME LIFESTYLES

Your thoughts will always determine your legacy.

1. Your thoughts produce your beliefs...
2. Your beliefs produce your feelings...
3. Your feelings produce your actions and habits...
4. Your actions and habits produce your lifestyle...

The most successful professional athletes implement the skill of positive inner-talk. They are said to decrease their inner-talk from 50,000 to 20,000 times or less per day, and more than sixty percent of the time their inner-talk is positive.

We as Christians have the absolute basis for truth, the Bible. Why not one-up these world-class athletes and increase our positive talk to eighty percent or more? And I am not promoting "positive thinking." I'm talking about "truthful thinking," within the context of a relationship with God.

AS YOU LOVE YOURSELF

Here's an interesting thought: *You'll spend more time with yourself than with anybody else in your whole life.* Besides God, of course. Did you know that how you think and relate to yourself determines how you relate to others?

If you...

- understand and accept who you are, it will enable you to be an understanding and gracious friend.
- affirm and encourage yourself, you will be a friend who empowers and motivates others.
- celebrate your own mini-victories throughout the day, you'll celebrate with others the little triumphs in their lives.
- discover the strengths and uniqueness God planted within you, you'll also begin to see the strength and beauty in others.
- value yourself as an important representative of your King, you'll begin to treat everyone around you with honor and value.
- allow yourself to freely express your thoughts, feelings, bitterness, fear and anxieties to God, you're likely to listen well to others since you're not "plugged up" with all of your own heart issues.

But, if you...

- condemn yourself, you'll be nitpicky and known as a faultfinder among your friends.
- are sarcastic regarding your mistakes and failures, you'll be the same with other people's shortcomings.
- ignore and disregard your strengths and successes, you'll most likely be a friend who ignores other people's victories.
- stuff down your hurts and anxieties, you're unlikely to be empathetic toward other peoples' difficulties.

This is the reason why the Bible teaches that the greatest principle of all is the "royal law:" Love your neighbor *AS* yourself (Galatians 5:14). The word *as* is a presumption and requirement for the previous commandment: Love others. After God, your most important relationship is with yourself. All other relationships are mirrors of these two.

YOUR SELF-TREATMENT IS A RESULT

So you're probably asking, *What's the first step in learning how to accept and encourage myself?*

Great question. You learn to accept and celebrate who you are when you experience God's love toward you, based on the truth of the Bible. It's not because you think it's a good idea, since you're so good looking. The Bible and practical observation teaches that the degree to which you can accept and love yourself will determine your ability to relate to others.

If you have never experienced and personalized the Father's love, you will not love yourself, and if you can't love yourself, you will not sincerely love others. You will never give out what you have never received. You will only be fabricating loving acts, motivated primarily by the fear of social rejection.

Let us love one another, for love comes from God. Everyone who loves has been born of God and knows God. Whoever does not love does not know God, because God is love. (1 John 4:7-8)

We know that we have passed from death to life, because we love our brothers. Anyone who does not love remains in death. (1 John 3:14)

Because God first loved you, you relate to yourself in a new light. Your belief of God's love for you is validated by how you relate to yourself, and ultimately how you love others.

PRESIDENT'S ASSISTANT

We value ourselves the same way we believe God values us. Let me give you an example.

Jerry has just been assigned to a new full time job as the assistant to the President of the United States. After all the initial jitters and anxiety over his new position, Jerry receives a call from a presidential advisor who instructs him, "You just do everything the President tells you."

This is the extent of his training.

When Jerry first meets the President, he is quite surprised at the warm and personal reception he receives. For the first few months, Jerry does absolutely nothing but follow the President to all his meetings, dinner parties and even to his daily exercise workouts.

From day one, Jerry notices that one of the Secret Service agents is always carrying a small cube of a box. The agent carries and protects this little box as if his life depends on it. Occasionally, the President takes the box into his private quarters during Jerry's absence. Jerry's curiosity is driving him crazy.

Even six months later, he's still just following the President around, doing nothing. But he's even more curious about the contents of the box. Is it jewelry? Is it money? Is it the button that controls the nuclear weapons? Whatever it is, it must be very important.

Eighteen long and grueling months pass, and then one day, the President looks at Jerry with a long, stern look, while holding the box in his hands. He says, "Jerry, starting today, you're going to be the person responsible for carrying and protecting this box." Jerry feels incredibly honored! At the same time, he's scared to death of such an enormous assignment. But he still doesn't know what's in the box, and he's too frightened to ask.

After six and half years of serving the President, Jerry finally retires. All those years he's cared for the box with the utmost protection, responsibility and integrity, faithfully executing this monumental task. But even to the last day, he doesn't know what the box contains.

Because the "box" is very important to the President, it became very important to Jerry.

Because he took his responsibility seriously, Jerry learned to treat the box in the same manner the President and the Secret Service agents did. He treated it with the utmost reverence, even though he had no idea what was in it. He was even willing to give up his life for it.

In the same way that Jerry valued the box because the President valued it, you value yourself because God values you. You talk to yourself in the same manner that you believe God talks to you. Even Jesus lived a life of love from the experience *He* had with His Father during His time on earth.

> As the Father has loved me, so have I loved you… A new command I give you: Love one another. As I have loved you, so you must love one another… Dear friends, since God so loved us, we also ought to love one another. (John 15:9, 13:34, 1 John 4:11)

The Lord tells us in eight different places in the Bible that we should love our neighbor *as* we love ourselves. The first step in accepting, approving and celebrating the uniqueness and beauty of those we meet is to accept, approve and celebrate who God designed *us* to be.

Do you know who you really are?

As a believer you are:

- an adopted royal child of the King of kings (Romans 8:15)
- forgiven (Ephesians 1:6-8)
- dearly loved (Colossians 3:12)
- given spiritual authority (Luke 10:19)
- capable through Christ who strengthens you (Philippians 4:13)
- gifted with power, love and sound mind (1 Timothy 1:7)
- God's workmanship (Ephesians 2:10)
- given direct access to the throne of God (Hebrews 4:14-16)
- righteous and holy (Ephesians 4:24)
- more than a conqueror (Romans 8:37)

If you heard that a man with all these traits was coming to your house for dinner, how would you treat him? Have you taken the time to really meditate on the truths above? They apply to you, if you are a believer *and* follower of Jesus.

Are you ready to treat and relate to yourself the way God does? In the next chapter, I want more than anything to introduce you to the real you, so that you will never again see yourself in the same way. My prayer is that you would see yourself as a person in whom God takes incredible delight, and that you will follow His example and treat yourself as He does.

SUMMARY

1. Your inner-talk is a result of your belief regarding how God thinks and talks to you.
2. How you relate to yourself is a result of how you see God relating to you.
3. How you relate to yourself determines how you relate to others.

DISCUSSION QUESTIONS

1. What do you think it means when Jesus said, "As you love yourself?"
2. What are some of the sarcastic or discouraging words you say to yourself?
3. Do you ever encourage and console yourself?

PRAYER

My Lord, please teach me how to love others as I love myself.
Please teach me how to love myself based on the truth of your Word.
Help me to see who I am in the same way that You have.

CHAPTER 12

HABIT #5:
CELEBRATE YOURSELF

As God Celebrates You

*It's surprising how many persons go through life
without ever recognizing that their feelings toward other
people are largely determined by their feelings toward
themselves, and if you're not comfortable within yourself,
you can't be comfortable with others.*
—SIDNEY J. HARRIS

I praise you because I am fearfully and wonderfully made.
—DAVID, PSALM 139:14

Did you know that your God celebrates who you are?
Celebrate means "to observe with ceremonies of respect, festivity, or rejoicing; to extol or praise; assign great importance to."

A few weeks ago I was at a church speaking on the subject of this book. After my message, I was involved in a conversation with one of the leaders of the church. Richard soberly shared his heart about the subject of my message.

"Mike, I completely understand what you mean about being gracious with ourselves. Except we need to realize that God can't always put up with our disobedience, ya know? We need to get our act together because God can only put up with so much."

I asked him, "Are you telling me that your main motivation for living and obeying Him is fear? Specifically, fear of His anger and disapproval?"

He answered without hesitation, "Why of course! Shouldn't we?"

Because of the lie Richard embraced, he justified his continued pattern of self-condemnation, which naturally spills over to everyone around him. He thought it was right to be hard on himself for his failures. I was sad for Richard, because he didn't understand that all of God's anger and irritation toward him was already unloaded on Jesus 2,000 years ago. He didn't understand that God desires a respectful fear towards Him, *not* a fear of His condemnation and anger.

> *God desires a respectful fear towards Him, not a fear of His condemnation and anger.*

> Therefore, there is now no condemnation for those who are in Christ Jesus. (Romans 8:1)

It's God's kindness that now motivate us to change, not His anger.

DO YOU LIKE YOURSELF?

Do you like who you are? Do you see yourself as a smart person? How do you deal with yourself when you make mistakes and/or fail?

Did you know that some people would like to go to the throne room of God and trade themselves in for a new body? What they don't realize is, when they get there, they would find that most everybody else is there desiring to trade themselves in as well.

Do you wonder why you think this way about yourself?

Satan wants to convince you that it's sufficient to know *about* God's love, but unnecessary to live as if God is crazy in-love with you. The father of lies doesn't want you to meditate on how much God delights in your unique God-given qualities.

Satan wants you to focus on what is three steps ahead—trying harder to be a better person—rather than basking in God's love and accepting yourself. Satan knows that if you focus on what is three steps ahead, it brings you to an endless cycle of failure and self-condemnation.

An overwhelming number of preachers in our day teach others to just try harder to bear fruit, and make them feel guilty for not trying enough. It has created a generation of guilt-ridden, fake people. Generally, we are a society of surface relationships where we go around saying, "How are you doing?" "Oh, I'm doing great," when all the while, our true interest toward others is only an inch deep.

In this way Satan has sneaked his lie into the family of God to enslave us with fear.

> For you did not receive a spirit that makes you a slave again to fear, but you received the Spirit of sonship. And by him we cry, "Abba, Father." (Romans 8:15)

AS YOU TREAT YOURSELF

Did you know that the more comfortable you are with yourself, the more comfortable you'll be with other people? And the more comfortable you are with others, the more comfortable they are with you. When you don't like yourself, chances are you are uncomfortable in public. When you don't feel valued by God, you will struggle with insecurity. At the core of insecurity is a heart that never found its way home to God's unconditional love.

Unless you stand on a firm foundation, believing and personalizing what God thinks and feels toward you, you can't take the next step of accepting and celebrating who you are.

When I say we need to celebrate ourselves, again, I don't mean to suggest being arrogant, conceited, or prideful. I'm simply suggesting that you look at yourself in the same way God does—as His highly valued child—who has been spared from, but truly deserve, the most unimaginable punishment and wrath known to mankind.

The Bible tells us that we should love others *as we love ourselves*. Do you ever wonder what our society would be like if we treated others the way we treat ourselves? My guess is that we would need to expand our prison facilities for half of the population.

What does it mean to *love ourselves?*

MY EXPERIENCE WITH CELEBRATING

I was really insecure growing up.

I remember thinking, "Wow, I wish I was as confident as all the other kids." It wasn't long before I realized I wasn't the only one who was insecure. But realizing the truth didn't help me to become more secure. At first I thought being secure just came with time and age, but I was wrong about that, too.

I knew God loved me; I just never truly believed it. Therefore, I didn't feel it. I struggled with *mental fear picturing*. This resulted in continual self-condemnation for failures and mistakes I made. I excused the way I treated myself because I reasoned that it motivated me to do better.

When I began this determined quest to learn the key to living the promised abundant life mentioned in the Bible, my life has never been the same. Now I'm actually experiencing the overwhelming love of God! Not to mention, I have never felt so free in all my life. Free to love and be loved. I am at rest with myself. I respect and honor who God made me to be.

I also have shocked myself how much more I smile as of late. I see myself being unusually patient towards people who in the past got on my nerves. I've enjoyed getting to know other people much more. I've also been surprised to see how much more people actually like me now.

Kristy and I often feel like we're not the same people we were in our early married years. It would take too long to explain what has happened in our marriage relationship since we've learned to accept and celebrate who we are in Christ. As a result, we have enjoyed and laughed with each other more than ever. We literally feel like we've undergone a heart transplant.

WHEN DID WE STOP CELEBRATING?

When a four-year-old tells you that she actually climbed up a little hill, we encourage her in her success. But if an adult tells you that he made three sales last night netting $400 per sale, you would likely challenge his arrogant tendencies.

At what age did we as a society decide to stop celebrating successes?

Most parents stop the praising and celebrating as the kids get older, and

At what age did we as a society decide to stop celebrating successes?

the family grows. This causes confusion and insecurity in a child's heart. In response, the child attempts to get the attention they were used to receiving, by taking drastic and often annoying measures. These drastic measures to get attention and approval, for some, will take them to the grave.

In contrast, I remember talking to a man named Brian who was a successful businessman. He made a lot of money and was well known in the executive world of business. I asked him what his key was to his success. He simply said, "My parents told me I could do anything."

This repetitive message from his parents made all the difference in his life.

REPROGRAM TO CELEBRATE

There's no way around it. The depth of your relationship with God will determine whether you'll continue down the same enslaving path of self-condemnation or embrace the beauty of celebrating your identity in Christ.

The key to reprogramming your mind is repetitive, biblically based inner-talk, rooted in what you've heard your Lord say to you. I say reprogramming because you already talk to yourself all the time, whether you believe it or not. You're doing it right now as you read this. I'm just encouraging you to *replace* your old pre-programmed messages with truth based inner-talk.

Countless research studies have conclusively proven that the content and frequency of what you say out loud will drastically change your life. In short, these messages must agree with what the Bible promises:

The tongue has the power of life and death, and those who love it will eat its fruit. (Proverbs 18:21)

Do not let this Book of the Law depart from your mouth; meditate on it day and night, so that you may be careful to do everything written in it. Then you will be prosperous and successful. (Joshua 1:8)

Fix these words of mine in your hearts and minds; tie them as symbols on your hands and bind them on your foreheads. Teach them to your children, talking about them when you sit at home and when you walk along the road, when you lie down and when you get up. (Deuteronomy 11:18-19)

The thalamus is the part of your brain that receives audio and visual information, the part that sorts and processes information. Research studies prove that repetitive words spoken to yourself are key to long-term and permanent change. Your thalamus is more likely to believe information when it is originating from your own mouth, than when you hear it from someone else.

This is a much-coveted biblical truth that thousands of successful sports psychologists and coaches have learned from the Bible and use to their advantage. Rarely will you find an Olympic gold medalist who hasn't harnessed the power of "self-encouragement."

Negative inner-talk, on the other hand, is worse than no talk at all. In 1987, pioneering psychologist Albert Ellis, PhD, identified general irrational beliefs that can interfere with athletes reaching their potential. They include statements such as: "If I don't do well, I'm an incompetent person," or "I must do well to gain the approval of others."[5]

In this game called life, what's at stake is much, much greater than simply winning a gold medal for your country.

Do you know what would happen to your life when you implement truthful inner-talk?

---

5. Psychology Today, May/June 2000.

FROM LEARNING DISABILITY TO GENIUS

Here's an example of a person who implemented the habit of encouraging inner-talk.

At age seven, John had a learning disability and was told that he would never read, write, or communicate normally. At fourteen, he dropped out of school, left his home and headed for the California coast. By seventeen, he ended up surfing the waves of Oahu's famous North Shore, where he almost died from strychnine poisoning.

His road to recovery led him to a doctor, a ninety-three-year-old man who changed John's life by encouraging him to say one simple statement every day: "*I am a genius, and I apply my wisdom.*" Inspired by his doctor, he has said these words every day of his life since that time.

John went on to go to college, earned his bachelor's degree from the University of Houston, and later earned his doctoral degree to be a chiropractor. Today, John is a very successful businessman, the author of fifty-four training programs and thirteen books. John spends the year traveling the world speaking and training others. Not bad for someone who was told he would never read, write or talk normally.

Your relationship with God will determine what you say to yourself.

Your relationship with God will determine what you say to yourself. What you say to yourself determines what you think. What you think and picture in your mind determines what you believe. What you believe determines how you eventually live.

ACTION POINTS

Are you ready to open the doors of your inner prison and release yourself to know and love God, to love yourself and to love others as you love yourself?

For you created my inmost being; you knit me together in my mother's womb. *I praise you because I am fearfully and wonderfully made*; your works are wonderful, I know that full well. My frame was not hidden from you when I was made in the secret place. When I was woven together in the depths of the earth, your eyes saw my unformed body. All the days ordained for me were written in your book before one of them came to be. (Psalm 139:13-16)

When Kristy and I embarked on this adventure of learning to celebrate, we had a hard time knowing where to start. At first we tried to fight all of our negative and defeated thoughts about ourselves. After a long and unsuccessful attempt to eliminate them, we realized they would never ever go away if we continued to follow the *elimination trap*.

The only to way to delete negative thoughts is to practice the *replacement principle* (repent). So, instead of fighting them, we decided to flush them out of our minds by repeating truth that we heard from our time alone with our heavenly Dad.

Here are some habits that you can implement to help you celebrate who you are:

1. Make a list of the things you like about yourself.

Compile a list of all the things that you like about yourself. Chances are you'll stumble across strengths and gifts that your Dad gave you. These are the very skills, gifts and talents that He will use to fulfill your personal mission here on earth.

Personally, I typed out my spiritual gifts and God-given strengths, printed them and taped them in front of my desk. This is a daily reminder to me of who I am. It helps me to have razor sharp focus on the tools that I have to fulfill my personal mission from my King. This exercise was extremely encouraging to me. It helped me to focus on how God sees me, and it encouraged me to build on what He has given me.

2. At the dinner table share five successes you've had that day.

Now, these don't have to be huge monumental things. We need to learn to celebrate ALL of our successes, not just those that the world deems important. Some examples are—I had tons of energy to do my work today; I forgave everyone I needed to forgive; I spent quality time with my kids; I cooked a healthy meal for my family tonight; I spoke well to myself today.

Our four-year-old daughter even participates in this exercise, and she loves it. Although her answers are much cuter than ours—I had fun reading library books; I'm happy because Jesus loves me so much; I liked having a craft time today.

After each one of us shares our successes, the rest of us cheer for that person and their personal triumphs.

Now some of you might think we're teaching our children to be boastful. Prideful boasting is a condition of the heart. Just because we share successes throughout the day doesn't mean it comes from a prideful heart. Instead, we use this time to teach our children about humility as well as celebrating and encouraging. The interesting thing about this is that the more I've learned to not only receive God's love and celebrate who I am, I've been way less likely to boast.

3. Make a point to keep in check all day about your inner-talk.

Kristy and I remind each other to be nice to ourselves. It really helps to have someone reminding you. At this point, our discernment level has increased to where we can see if the other is following the perfectionism lie, or if we're being too hard on ourselves just by our facial expression.

Since we're not always aware of our own thinking, we listen for other personal security alarms: our emotions, health and how we relate to others.

4. Focus on taking care of yourself better.

Part of loving yourself is actually caring for what you need emotionally and physically. Kristy and I are careful not to neglect our needs in any way. When we feel like we are getting down on ourselves, we take time to get alone and meditate on how much God loves us. When we're starting to become fatigued from reaching out to others, we rest. It's that simple. It's called implementing healthy boundaries. Jesus did it, and we should follow His example (Matthew 26:36, Mark 1:35).

It's the same idea taught by airline flight attendants. They tell you that you should put your oxygen mask on first in an emergency, for by doing so, you'll be able to help others. When you don't, you're useless to everyone.

5. Stand in front of the mirror and do the Breakthrough Declarations.

I want to encourage you to do these *Breakthrough Declarations*, right after your daily time with the Lord, or whenever it works best for you. People have been changed and healed by saying the words below. Say them privately, in front of a mirror—with lots of emotion and conviction, with a smile and with all your heart.

(Your name), your God adores and enjoys you immensely. You don't ever have to be perfect to be approved by your heavenly Dad. He is absolutely crazy about you! He is always pursuing to have a deeper friendship with you. He is waiting patiently to listen to your heart. He is happy with you right here and right now. Today, you will believe what He says.

(Your name), your God will always provide for all of your needs. He watches over you every minute of every day. He is bigger than any problem that you'll ever encounter. He is the one who split the Red Sea. He gave David victory over Goliath. He will do exceedingly and abundantly above all that you could imagine.

(Your name), your heavenly Dad believes in you. He is proud of you. He accepts and approves of you just as you are. He has forgiven all your mistakes and failures in the past, present and future. Celebrate His love all the days of your life. You are free! You are an overcomer and a conqueror for the Lord.

(Your name), I forgive you for all of your failures, just as God has. Your heavenly Dad has creatively made you. There will never be another like you. You are an original, a unique workmanship created for a mission only you can fulfill. Today, I celebrate who you are.

(The above *Breakthrough Declarations* are available in a postcard [4x6-inch] version for your convenience so you can put it up on your mirror or take it with you if you're out and about. If you would like to purchase one for yourself or for your friends and family, please go to www.Michael Trillo.com)

The first time I said the *Breakthrough Declarations* to myself, I couldn't finish them. I couldn't look myself in the eyes, because I didn't completely believe what I was saying. When I finally did finish, I wept like a baby.

I was unbelievably touched by the truth of what I was saying. I discovered that I haven't respected or treated myself with the same love God has given me. Looking at yourself in the mirror is the ultimate test of whether you have moved from just knowing to truly believing. It is a personal lie detector test.

I have noticed that I feel much more calm, to which Kristy agrees. The funny thing is, I never knew I needed to *be* calm! She says I'm much more centered and gracious toward others now than I was before. The ironic thing about this is I never *tried* to be calm, centered or gracious.

It is a result. "If a man remains in me and I in him, he will bear much fruit" (John 15:5).

This exercise has spilled over into every area of my life. Once a week, I play basketball with a bunch of friends from church. When I play really well, I catch myself saying, "Man, that was a good looking shot!" Don't panic, I only say it in my head. As odd as it may sound, I have become my biggest encourager. This encouragement has spilled over into my words with others. I find myself wanting to support and encourage others, and it doesn't even take any effort.

It is a result. "If a man remains in me and I in him, he will bear much fruit" (John 15:5).

I can't imagine ever dropping this habit. I can't believe I used to "beat myself up" for mistakes. I can't believe that I used to live that way! No wonder I did the same towards others.

Now don't get me wrong—the heavy fist of guilt and condemnation still knocks at my door and occasionally sneaks in. But when it does, I take a quick inventory of my emotions and health, and I resist and praise (James 4:7-8). At this point of my life, failures are opportunities to say, "I'm sorry" to my Dad. Then I thank Him for showing me my mistake, praise Him and celebrate His forgiveness and finally, I take the necessary action to stop the mistake I'm doing.

KRISTY'S BREAKTHROUGH DECLARATIONS
(KRISTY WRITING)

My experience was an eye-opener for me. I discovered that when I am face to face with myself, looking into my eyes, I can't lie to myself. I realized that I didn't believe these truths that I was trying to state. Inevitably, all my issues with myself surfaced and spilled out.

I came face to face with how uncomfortable I was to maintain eye contact with myself in the mirror. And I don't mean eye contact like when I put on make-up in the morning or brush my teeth. I mean really looking deep into my eyes and reading my heart.

I had to force myself to get past how stupid I felt saying these things. I was surprised to find that I couldn't say these truths without crying. Eventually, while saying the declarations, I felt this relaxing peace come over me and all my muscles that had been tense, just relaxed in a matter of minutes.

I pondered why this was, and asked the Holy Spirit to help me understand why I felt such peace. I came to realize it was because I was hearing words I had never heard from myself before. Then I thought about how we are with ourselves. Why is it that we have a tendency to treat others the way we want them to treat us? Could it be that all we are looking for is "another me" to love ourselves? Is it because we long so badly to be accepted by ourselves, but mostly what we hear from ourselves is rejection and condemnation?

It was a huge breakthrough for me to adopt this practice. I will never be the same again.

COMMENTS REGARDING "THE DECLARATIONS"

I want to cover a couple of comments that I've heard from those who have done this exercise:

1. "I feel silly when I do this."

Chances are, what you're really saying is that you're uncomfortable with yourself, and you have difficulty receiving, even from yourself. Remember— you're either celebrating or condemning yourself. There's no third option.

Choosing not to celebrate yourself is a choice to continue in self-condemnation. When you don't choose to celebrate, it's because you don't see yourself the way God does.

The fact that you have such a hard time finishing it (or even starting it) is a tell-tale sign that you need to implement this practice. I promise that you'll never be the same. This exercise has contributed enormously to launching me to live the abundant life promised in the Bible.

2. "I don't believe what I'm saying."

Doing this exercise contributes in transforming your heart by the renewing of your mind (Romans 12:2). It doesn't make sense for you to wait until you actually believe it before you say it out loud. This is like saying, "I can't believe some of the teachings of the Bible, so I'm going to stop reading the Bible." The repetition of these truths will convince your heart to believe, not the other way around. Remember—you're already talking to yourself. It's just a matter of changing the content to be more truth-based.

After thirty to forty days of consistently doing this, you'll notice that your negative inner-talk will go down significantly. The very first sign of change will be your treatment of others. You'll begin to discover and tell others the good character qualities you see in them. When you talk with people, you'll be aware of God's implanted strength in them and their uniqueness.

The more passion and frequency you have in practicing this exercise, the more powerful the change you'll experience. Heightened emotions and repetition speed up the process of the growth of your dendrites.

Also, if you need to, please feel free to change the wording to better fit your personality and style. I change it around depending on what I need to hear that day. I have grown to respect, honor and really like myself. I now appreciate how original and special I truly am before my Dad.

What would your life be like if everyday was a celebration?

SUMMARY

1. You have inner-talk going on all day long.
2. Your life patterns are a result of your repetitious inner-talk.
3. You treat yourself the way you believe God treats you.
4. You treat others the way you treat yourself.
5. When you don't love yourself, you'll have difficulty loving others.
6. Repetitious and biblically-based inner-talk reprograms your mind.

DISCUSSION QUESTIONS

1. What are the top three self-defeating comments you say to yourself?
2. The way you treat others is indicative of how you treat yourself. What have you learned about yourself by how you talk to others?
3. What are your thoughts about how David encouraged himself throughout the book of Psalm?

PRAYER

*Lord, help me to relate and talk to myself the way You do.
Help me to take seriously the responsibility of treating myself with the
utmost respect and care. Help me celebrate myself daily, and protect
me from any self-hatred or prideful tendencies. Thank You that
I am uniquely created for a purpose that no one else can ever fulfill.
Thank You that You delight in me!*

CHAPTER 13

KNOW AND LOVE OTHERS

As You Love Yourself

Love is saying, "I feel differently," instead of, "You're wrong."
—UNKNOWN

*The people who are lifting the world onward and upward
are those who encourage more than they criticize.*
—ELIZABETH HARRISON

Today, there is a miracle greater than signs and wonders.

Back in the Old Testament, the Israelites got to see Moses part the Red Sea. They saw Elijah's triumphant victory over the prophets of Baal. They saw little David beat up a giant. They saw Abraham and Sarah have a child at a ridiculously old age.

They saw Daniel survive an encounter with multiple "kings of the jungle" when he was thrown into the den of lions. They saw Moses perform ten miraculous signs. They saw God miraculously provide manna and quail in the wilderness. They saw Jericho's wall come crashing down after a single shout. They saw the sun and moon stand still for a day.

In the New Testament, people saw Jesus turn water into wine. They saw countless healings. They saw food multiply right before their eyes. They saw people raised from the dead. They saw Jesus come up from the grave. They saw Peter perform nine miracles, and the apostle Paul do eleven miracles. They saw Jesus *and* Peter (a mere man) walk on water.

Do you ever wish you could live a supernatural life? You can!

But did you know there's something greater?

I have a proposition for you. There's a miracle that's more powerful than any supernatural event that goes against reason and the laws of physics. It has been proven to change people's hearts more drastically than any superpower act. And it's available to anyone—including you.

Especially you.

The nation of Israel saw with their own eyes, all the miracles God performed before Pharaoh. They walked on dry ground through the Red Sea, with a wall of water on their right and on their left (Exodus 14:22,29). They saw how God provided throughout the forty years in the desert. They even saw Moses' shining countenance after he'd been with God.

There's a miracle that's more powerful than any supernatural event

But in spite of all these signs and wonders, do you know how many true believers Moses had out of over two million people?

Two—Joshua and Caleb.

It has been proven repeatedly that mighty miracles do not compel people to believe and follow God. So, God decided to add a twist to His *rescue mission*.

He lovingly invested in twelve ordinary and teachable God-seekers.

He showed the utmost personal love and intimacy toward His students when He humbly washed their feet (John 13:4-17), told them that He loved them (John 13:34) and called them His personal friends (John 15:14). The result? These twelve men started the greatest revolution the world has ever seen and will ever see; it's still continuing today with unparalleled momentum.

The disciples were never the same after they personally experienced the miraculous power of Jesus' love and friendship. This intimate encounter with Jesus drastically changed these men's lives. As a result of these twelve very ordinary but transformed men, this planet has never been the same.

So, what does this have to do with you today?

If you're a businessperson, parent, student, or especially if you're in the ministry—the most powerful miracle you can perform today is to love others unconditionally. It sounds too simple, doesn't it? Yet, we know it is easier to say the words than it is to actually love without any strings attached. To love with unconditional love is the greatest miracle you will ever undertake.

This incredible miracle is only made available to those who have received and personalized God's love. We love others because God first loved us.

Jesus said in John 13:35 that all men will "know that you are My disciples..."

Not by:

- walking on water
- having a dynamite TV ministry
- being a powerful speaker or preacher
- knowing all the answers from the Bible
- striving for perfection and following all the rules
- levitating in mid air

No! He said that all men will know that you are My disciples...

...*if you love one another.*

Apparently, love is to be the most powerful evidence available, and it is virtually impossible to fabricate on our own. This is not an either/or proposition between miracles and love. I'm all for living a life full of both. Between the two, love is greater.

> If I speak in the tongues of men and of angels, but have not love, I am only a resounding gong or a clanging cymbal. If I have the gift of prophecy and can fathom all mysteries and all knowledge, and if I have a faith that can move mountains, but have not love, I am nothing. If I give all I possess to the poor and surrender my body to the flames, but have not love, I gain nothing...And now these three remain: faith, hope and love. But the greatest of these is love. (1 Corinthians 13:1-3, 13)

In 2 Timothy 3:1-5, Paul warns Timothy:

> There will be terrible times in the last days. People will be lovers of themselves, lovers of money, boastful, proud, abusive, disobedient to their parents, ungrateful, unholy, without love, unforgiving, slanderous, without self-control, brutal, not lovers of the good...

Today, we live in a dark world of selfishness and evil. But in darkness, it doesn't take much to bring a brilliant glimmer of light. The love we receive and experience from God ushers that glimmer of light into our dark world.

Jesus said: ...*I did not come to judge the world, but to save it* (John 12:47). His strategy for saving was not by condemning us and telling us all our faults, but rather He chose the life-changing path of love.

In the same way, we show His love by living out daily habits that center around loving others—not by judging others. God's love...

- graciously accepts people just the way they are.
- consistently encourages and empowers others.
- asks someone how they really are doing, and then listens as they share their heavy heart.
- generously gives money to those in need.
- donates time to serve the widows, poor and the fatherless.
- writes an encouraging and timely note to someone in need.

Each of us desperately longs for a loving touch. It's much more powerful than any miracle we might see.

Loving others is not a natural tendency for any human being. We don't have the natural resource, loving nature, or internal tendency to love others. Loving others without personally experiencing love from God is an impossible undertaking. There's absolutely nothing inside of us inclined to be loving. Nada. Loving others involves a mandatory supernatural relational experience. It's also a result of learning to love ourselves.

There's absolutely nothing inside of us inclined to be loving.

How many times do you fabricate a loving act because you're worried how you'll look if you choose not to? How many times do you give to others only because there is a tally you have to cross off to be "even?" Regarding love as a "duty," will only result in exhaustion.

Am I now trying to win the approval of men, or of God? Or am I trying to please men? If I were still trying to please men, I would not be a servant of Christ. (Galatians 1:10)

So far, you've learned about the daily habit of forgiveness to free your-self to move forward. Then you learned that the first step necessary to move forward is to learn how to receive God's love. Once you're able to receive, you can press the pedal to the floor, pursuing your relationship with God and living a life of praise and gratitude. And finally you've learned the art of how to celebrate yourself the way God does.

The next two habits will allow you to daily live out this new love you've experienced from God and yourself. They're part of the Royal Law that tells us to love others *AS* we love ourselves. Though there are many ways we can express love, I believe these next habits are two of the most powerful ways you can live out a life of love.

PRAYER

*Lord, thank You so much that You're
continually pursuing my heart,
desiring for me to receive all of Your love.
I trust that You will help me transfer Your
love to all those around me.*

CHAPTER 14

HABIT #6: UNDERSTANDING

Celebrating Our Differences

Good understanding wins favor,
but the way of the unfaithful is hard.
—PROVERBS 13:15

When both parties are trying to be understood,
neither party is really listening.
—STEPHEN COVEY

Being misunderstood is extremely hurtful.
Understand: "to perceive and comprehend the nature of; to know thoroughly by close contact or experience; to grasp or comprehend the meaning intended."

Have you ever met anyone who's really different from you? You know, the type of person who dresses, talks, smells, lives, or believes differently? You probably have a long list of individuals in your head right now, don't you? What do you usually call these people who are so different from you?

When I was young, if someone was even slightly different from me, I had a special name for them: Weird.

As far as I was concerned, everyone who was not like me was weird. I have noticed that since those teen years, not much has changed. The only difference that adulthood brings is that now we call people weird behind their backs, rather than to their faces.

How many times have you left a social gathering and said these words to your spouse or friends while driving off... "Did you see...? Can you believe what he...? That guy/girl is so weird! Why did he/she say that...? I don't understand why he/she does weird things like that..."

Ever hear yourself talk like this? Ever hear others talk like this? If you catch yourself saying, "I don't understand...!" it's probably because you *don't* understand. Do you wonder why you don't? Ever wonder why you even say those words in the first place?

What you really mean every time you say, "I don't understand...!" is, "I don't understand why they're not acting or talking like I would, because if I were in their shoes, I would act and talk differently." In short, it doesn't make sense to you that they live differently than you do.

With only rare exceptions, we tend to put our guard up and close off from those who are different from us. It's easier to put up a wall than to try to get to know who they really are inside, to understand why they do what they do and to truly enjoy their uniqueness.

Have you ever felt like people thought you were the "weird" one? Think back to the last time this happened to you. How did it feel? Did it cause pain? Did you have imaginary conversations where you explained to them in great length why you did what you did and said what you said, so they could finally *understand* and accept you?

Satan wants us to be separated and isolated from others. To this end, he urges us to make quick assumptions and accusations about other peoples' intentions and preferences, rather than simply to understand and accept them.

On the other hand, God wants us to passionately pursue a loving relationship with others the same way He did with us. Unlike Satan, God's goal is to bring unity to His family. To this end, He wants us to understand and love each other.

We desire to be understanding toward others because our Lord Jesus first understood us.

> For we do not have a high priest who is unable to sympathize
> with our weaknesses, but we have one who has been tempted in
> every way, just as we are—yet was without sin. (Hebrews 4:15)

For this reason he had to be made like his brothers in every way, in order that he might become a merciful and faithful high priest in service to God… (Hebrews 2:17)

MISUNDERSTANDING INTENTIONS

It's easy for us to misunderstand the intentions of someone else.

The most common way we misunderstand other people is in regard to their intentions. This accusatory habit and tendency originates with Satan.

The most common way we misunderstand other people is in regard to their intentions.

For years, I fancied myself as one who could grasp a person's meaning mid-sentence instead of waiting for him to finish speaking. I've since learned that it's easy to misunderstand when we don't completely listen. It's much easier to interrupt or define words according to our definition, rather than trying to understand what the other person really means.

I've lost track of the times I've interrupted Kristy and got upset at what she said, only to hear her say, "If you had allowed me to finish, you would have learned that that's not what I meant."

I also struggled with presuming the intentions of others. Next time you're in a group situation, take time to listen to conversations going on around you. You'll be amazed how often you'll hear someone presume they know someone else's intentions. These presumptions are often mentioned casually, using softer words lest it comes across as blatant slander and accusation:

- "She just wears those clothes to get attention"—when in reality, she is naturally creative and likes to be fashionable.
- "He shared that verse to show off his Bible knowledge"—when in reality, he's excited to bless others by sharing what he's learned in the Bible.
- "He's telling me this to sell me something"—when in reality, he only desires to help you.

- "She tells me to go the other direction because she's just trying to control me"—when in reality, she's trying to protect you.
- "He says, 'hi' to people because he's just trying to be popular"—when in reality, he's a sincerely positive and friendly person.

A Thirty-Year Misunderstanding

What happens when you choose to live a life of presuming and accusing rather than listening and understanding? I heard the following story from a speaker, and it demonstrates the destructive consequences of misunderstanding another's intention.

Even at a young age, Dave was already a world-class salesman. One summer day after selling $300 worth of chocolates for a fundraiser, he placed all $300 in cash in a jar in his room. Several days later, he came home from school to find the jar empty.

Since he lived alone with his mom, he blamed her for taking the money. When she came home from work that day, Dave lashed out at her and accused her of taking the money. She responded by slapping his face, and because her ring was turned upside down, he started bleeding.

Dave ran away that day, and he's been running ever since. He's been to forty different countries in his quest to escape his problems. From the day of the incident, Dave vowed he would never trust women, especially with money.

Nearly thirty years later, he decided to make it right with his mom. He called her and asked what happened to the money in the jar. She said, "Well, your friend next door came over the day before and asked if he could look for something in your room. He was only in there for a few minutes, but after he left I wondered if he stole some of that money. When I counted the money in the jar, it was only $290. I went next door to talk to his mom. She checked his jean pockets, and sure enough, she found the ten dollars in his pocket. So, I added it to your money and placed it all in an envelope and put it in your closet."

Dave was appalled to realize that this thirty-year misunderstanding had caused him an unreasonable amount of mistrust toward women, not to mention needless anger and separation from his mom for thirty years. What a tragic story. Dave lived a thirty-year span of unnecessary pain because he made an erroneous presumption regarding his mom's intentions, and he never gave her a chance to explain the truth.

PREFERENCES AND CONVICTIONS

There are two concepts I would like to define for you: *preferences* and *convictions.*

- *Preference*—favorable bias; the act of choosing based on a certain liking for something or someone above another.
- *Conviction*—a fixed or strong belief; something believed or accepted as true by a person.

Let's see how preferences and convictions are lived out in our lives.

Preferences

It's very common for us as Christians to confuse biblical truths with preferences. When we perceive our preferences as truth, it results in judging those who don't agree with us.

For instance, you might like the color red, and I might like the color blue. You might like your home to be loud and chaotic, while I appreciate silence in mine. You might enjoy classical music, and I might like jazz. You might like hockey, and I might prefer basketball. It doesn't make either one of us right or wrong, bad or good.

It's very common for us as Christians to confuse biblical truths with preferences.

It hurts me to admit this, but I've lost track of how many times I've judged people for their preferences. In the past, I have judged others for being lazy, disorganized, poor financial managers, being too poor or rich, talking too much or too little, being arrogant, etc. The list goes on and on. I did this because I did the same thing with myself. I didn't know how to accept, forgive, enjoy, or celebrate myself. But since I've started walking this new path of self-acceptance, I've grown to appreciate and celebrate other people more than ever before.

When I've been on the receiving end of judgment, the times that would wound me most were those where I was misunderstood and rejected by others for my personal preferences, my personality, or my convictions. The people who I most often struggled to forgive were those who misunderstood me and refused to accept me for who I am.

God has made each of us special with a unique set of personality traits that include: talents, skills, humor, passion, dreams, etc. Each of us is an irreplaceable original, not a manufactured copy of four hundred other people. We should seek to deeply get to know, accept and sincerely enjoy each other!

> Accept one another, then, just as Christ accepted you, in order to bring praise to God. (Romans 15:7)

Convictions

Some people believe we should never celebrate Valentine's Day because of its pagan origin, while others think Valentine's Day is the most special day of the year. Some people think jeans are straight from Satan. Others think jeans are the best thing since sliced bread. Some think it's fine to occasionally drink alcohol and listen to secular music, while others think such a lifestyle is a front row ticket to hell.

It's only human nature to try to align everyone else's convictions with our own. So, what do you do when you come across people who think differently than you do?

> Accept him whose faith is weak, without passing judgment on disputable matters. (Romans 14:1)

> Do not judge, or you too will be judged. (Matthew 7:1)

Some are afraid to let others be different because they have to be in control. Others believe there is only one right way to do everything, and it's their sole purpose on earth to correct all that's wrong with the rest of us. But this is simply another form of perfectionism. No matter what the reason, a critical spirit is based from a poisonous, perfectionistic mindset. You need to recognize the menacing and destructive grip of perfectionism when you see it, and then you should run from it like the plague.

THOUGH IT COST ALL YOU HAVE

A few years ago, I remember discussing this passage with Kristy:

> Wisdom is supreme; therefore get wisdom. *Though it cost all you have*, get understanding. (Proverbs 4:7)

I told her that besides learning how to listen to the Holy Spirit more, I wanted understanding more than anything, and I didn't care how much it cost. I had no idea what was to come over the next couple years. This was the seed that birthed the stressful roller coaster ride I shared with you in chapter five.

When the Lord saw the change we wanted in our hearts, He rearranged our life to the point that it cost us almost all we had. We gave up so many of our possessions, pride and comfort. But in return we gained more in understanding and spiritual riches than we ever expected. We often discussed the many ways we had judged others. I can't even count the times we said to each other, "Remember when we used to judge others for this? Now we're experiencing the exact same thing."

Now we understand.

At one time in our life, we were living the good life, successfully working at a great sales job of seven years. We owned two houses—one to live in and one rental house that gave us extra monthly income. We had two new vehicles paid for in full. To say the least, we were comfortable. But then the Lord wisely chose to take that lifestyle, and give us *real* life in return. Looking back, I would never trade what I experienced for the life of "comfort" I once had.

167

I once heard a friend say, "Sometimes God has to clear the table so He can set it Himself." Not too long ago, everything we owned fit into the trunk of our truck, along with a few suitcases. The Lord had to show me that my quest for understanding had a price.

My quest for understanding had a price.

He showed us that our convictions are just that—*our convictions.* Everyone who loves and obeys God is going down the path as God leads. We won't all experience the same path or convictions, and that's okay. Kristy and I are so grateful that He opened our eyes and helped us to be more understanding. We will forever praise Him for it!

THE PAIN OF MISUNDERSTANDING

The greatest emotional pain comes from being misunderstood. With no exception, all of my imaginary conversations involve me convincing another person who has misunderstood me. Misunderstanding is at the center of family conflicts and break ups.

One of the most eye-opening moments in my life occurred a few years ago when I read Stephen Covey's book, *7 Habits of Highly Effective Families.* The title for chapter five is: *Seek First to Understand…Then to Be Understood.*

After reading this chapter, my mind was awhirl with thoughts, reflecting on the previous years of our marriage. I looked back and reflected on the root cause of our frequent and unnecessary "lengthy discussions." I was surprised to discover that virtually every "discussion" was based on a misunderstanding of each other's intentions or the meaning of words. Since that time, we changed our objective for our "discussions." Our previous objective was to discover who was right and who was wrong and to determine a winner. Since then, we've changed our objective to: *seek first to understand.* Now we choose to listen while giving the other person a chance to explain. We then repeat it back to clarify and make sure we understand.

ACTION POINTS

1. Listen Completely

Make it a goal not to interrupt, especially your family members or spouse, since they are the easiest to take for granted. When you do interrupt, do your best to apologize for it. This is one of many "rules of engagement" we keep in our family.

> He who answers before listening, that is his folly and his shame.
> (Proverbs 18:13)

2. Ask the Intention and Meaning of Words

Oftentimes you'll discover after a few hours of "discussion" that you have entirely different objectives. And when your objectives are different, you'll never arrive at the same destination. So, at the beginning of each disagreement, Kristy and I usually ask each other the question, "What's your objective in asking this question?" I can't tell you how many times this has shortened unnecessary "discussions."

> A fool finds no pleasure in understanding but delights in airing his own opinions. (Proverbs 18:2)

Also, when we hear a specific word or phrase we're unsure of, we ask, "What do you mean by this word or that phrase?" Often the answer surprises us. After which we breathe a sigh of relief that we asked before we lost self control.

Another good way to implement this principle is by the *five magical words*—'So what you're saying is…" We will understand more clearly by repeating back to people what we hear them say. It not only gives us a chance to understand, but it also helps them to feel validated.

People absolutely love it when someone actually desires to understand their heart.

3. Protect Other People's Preferences

Anytime I'm in a conversation and I hear someone judging someone else for how they dress, talk, walk, live, etc., I usually say, "Yeah, everybody's different. We don't know the story behind that person."

> The lips of the righteous know what is fitting, but the mouth of the wicked only what is perverse. (Proverbs 10:32)

The problem with some of us is that we have become so slick with the softer words we use to slander and judge other people that we don't even realize we're doing it.

4. Give the Benefit of the Doubt

When I'm in a conversation and someone starts to make presumptions about *other people's intentions,* I try to protect that other person's reputation by saying, "Well, we can't say 'they're trying to be...' since we don't really know their heart." At this point the accused person's reputation is at stake, and I feel a strong need to protect it.

> A good name is more desirable than great riches; to be esteemed is better than silver or gold. (Proverbs 22:1)

When you make presumptions about other people, there's always more at stake than what you see. What you're really doing is gossiping and slandering another person. You're bringing false accusations. You also lose the trust of the person in front of you, since they know that you have just as much potential to talk behind their backs.

I once talked negatively about the boyfriend of a girl I was advising. While we were talking, she happened to accidentally call her boyfriend on her cell. Inevitably, the guy I was slandering heard everything I said. When I found out about it, I wanted to shrivel up and die, especially since I was making presumptions about a person I barely knew. Later, I got to know this person much better, and I was ashamed when I learned he was a really good-hearted guy. He was one of the people I talked about in chapter six that I have had to ask forgiveness from.

Interestingly enough, a similar experience happened a few years later, except that this time, I was the one who accidentally overheard myself being slandered from a phone conversation. Now I understand how it feels.

He who conceals his hatred has lying lips, and whoever spreads slander is a fool. (Proverbs 10:18)

5. Accept People Where They Are

More often than not, we desire to change other people's fruits and behaviors rather than changing the root cause of the behavior. If they have embraced a lie, they are deeply hurting. Instead of only judging their behavior, we should encourage them to find love from God and develop a friendship with Him. Changing the root is the best way to produce permanent change in behavior.

The truth is, we have absolutely no idea regarding another person's motives or the reason they do what they do. If we would first ask questions and let them share, they might release a flood of unexpressed *heart suffering* that has been festering for days, months, or even years—wounds that have been screaming for a listening ear.

> *More often than not, we desire to change other people's fruits and behaviors rather than changing the root cause of the behavior.*

With hardly any exception, each of us is dying to meet someone who will take a personal interest in us and actually listen to our story. If you're a person who's thinking, "I can't listen to someone ramble for more than five minutes," chances are your heart is filled with heaviness that you've never vented to the Lord. And if that's the case, don't work on being a better listener. Learn to better share your heart with your God. He wants to hear everything you have to say.

When you've been heard, you'll be ready to listen.

When I first met my Hero, the Lord Jesus, I started working construction and maintenance at my church full time. One particular guy named

171

Steve Waterman stood out to me. He volunteered with church maintenance. Though I was a rough-around-the-edges sixteen-year-old and a new
Christian, he always encouraged me and made me feel like a giant, able to
conquer anything that got in my way.

Steve never made me feel condemned in any way, even though I was extremely raw with my social skills. Instead, he was always interested in what
I had to say. Every moment we spent time together, I felt he accepted me
and understood me. I promised myself that when I grew up, I wanted to be
just like him.

His acceptance was a miraculous gift. I got to see Jesus in the flesh. It
enabled me to know and serve my God better. Consequently, my bad behaviors slowly began to fall away.

6. Say, "I Understand"

Have you ever heard people who constantly repeat themselves, even their
jokes?

I've asked many people why they often repeat themselves, and without
exception, they say it's because they feel like they're not being understood.
Since I've incorporated the words "I understand" in my conversations, I've
been absolutely amazed at how encouraged people feel.

Recently, Kristy and I were babysitting for some friends. When it came
time to go to bed, their son started crying. I knelt down by his bed and tried
to calm him.

He kept saying, "I miss my daddy!" The more I asked him to stop crying and calm down, the louder he cried. The Holy Spirit then reminded me
that everyone has a deep longing to be loved, and the best way to help
people feel loved is to help them feel understood.

This includes young children.

I then sat next to him and repeated back what he was saying, "So you
miss daddy, huh?" He immediately stopped crying and locked his eyes on
mine. "Yeah, I miss daddy."

I said, "I'm really sorry. You really do miss daddy, don't you?"

He said, "Yeah, I miss daddy. I wish he was here." "What do you miss about daddy?"

He said, "I miss having daddy here."

Hugging him I said, "I totally understand. When I was little, I used to miss my daddy really bad every time he was gone."

He looked at me and smiled, as if to say—*thank you for understanding*. In seconds, his voice quieted and he started to relax. I told him his daddy would be back soon. I made him laugh a few times, told him stories and *Everyone wants to be understood.* I eventually reassured him that if he needed anything, to come get us. He went straight to sleep.

Everyone wants to be understood.

7. Know and Enjoy Others

When I was a youth leader, I took a group of high school kids on a short-term mission trip to the Philippines. I was shocked at how relational the Filipino people were, in comparison to Americans. It was a total culture shock, although it was particularly fulfilling at the same time.

The first night I was there, I met a guy about my age named Joe. For three hours we shared each other's spiritual journeys, personal calling and ministry experience. After talking, we prayed together and hugged. It was as if we had known each other all our lives. We talked at a level of intimacy and connection that I wasn't used to. My heart was brimming with joy and strength after we shared our hearts with each other.

How good and pleasant it is when brothers live together in unity! (Psalm 133:1)

My prayer is that you would learn to accept, protect, enjoy and celebrate your differences with others. I propose that this is only possible when you have done the same with yourself, and when you've experienced it with your relationship with God.

SUMMARY

1. Misunderstanding other people's intentions has become a norm in our society.
2. Misunderstanding is the number one cause of family pain.
3. You love others by accepting and respecting their differing preferences and convictions.
4. Listening and asking other people's intentions and meanings help avoid unnecessary judging.
5. You need to protect other people's reputation and give them the benefit of the doubt.

DISCUSSION QUESTIONS

1. What are things that you judge people for the most?
2. Would your friends and family say that you're a good listener?
3. Would you consider yourself an understanding person? What would your friends and family say?

PRAYER

*Lord, thank You so much that You have been an
understanding and accepting Dad to me.
Thank You that You're helping me to become accepting of myself as well.
Please help me to become as loving as possible towards others.
I want to become an understanding and accepting person so
that I would be able to live out what I've experienced with You.*

CHAPTER 15

HABIT #7:
ENCOURAGE OTHERS

Unleashing Life Words

*I have yet to find a man, however exalted his station,
who did not do better work and put forth greater effort
under a spirit of approval than under a spirit of criticism.*
—CHARLES SCHWAB

*There is more hunger for love and appreciation
in this world than for bread.*
—MOTHER TERESA

Deep down, everybody wants to be encouraged.
Encourage: "To inspire with hope, courage, or confidence; to give support to; to make someone feel more confident."

A management consulting firm surveys 200 companies every year to discover what motivates employees. It's no surprise that the number one motivation for employees is appreciation, number two is feeling "in" on things, and number three is being understood. The truth is, these management gurus are simply agreeing with the foundational truths of the Bible.

Deep down, we all have a profound need to be loved. One of the ways that we feel most loved and appreciated is through the encouraging power of words.

Encourage one another and build each other up, just as in fact
you are doing… And let us consider how we may spur one

another on toward love and good deeds. (1 Thessalonians 5:11, Hebrews 10:24)

Encouragement is one of the greatest gifts we can give another human being. Our heavenly Dad wants us to pursue a loving relationship with oth-

Encouragement is one of the greatest gifts we can give another human being.

ers just the way He does. When we encourage others, we share words of strength that continue to echo for hours.

Sometimes for generations.

Do you have an idea how powerful words are? Allow me to share some remarkable facts.

HOME COURT ADVANTAGE

If you don't believe in the power of encouragement, go watch your local professional basketball team and see the power of words in action.

I absolutely love watching NBA basketball games. I am a huge fan of the Seattle Sonics since I live in Seattle. One of the most interesting observations I've had at basketball games involves this whole concept called "home court advantage." The home court advantage occurs when a sports team plays in their home city against a team from another city. One study showed that the home court advantage in basketball produced a winning percentage of 66.77 percent in the playoffs and 64.45 percent in the regular season.

Do you ever wonder why this winning percentage holds true across the board, in every sport?

Typically, the visiting team is introduced first, followed by a round of boos. When it's time to introduce the home team, the announcer completely changes the tone and volume of his voice to one of excitement and suspenseful anticipation.

The regular lights go off, with large spotlights focusing on each player as he is introduced. All the while, the music in the background heightens the moment. This is when the crowd stands up, clapping and yelling at the top of their lungs—cheering for their home team. There are cardboard signs throughout the arena with words of encouragement to cheer on the home team players. You can feel the electricity and power of support in the air.

Incredible as it may seem, hearing and seeing the fans cheer, makes a huge difference to these grown men, as unemotional as they might try to appear. Being cheered on changes their thinking process, which in turn changes their performance.

While watching the NBA Finals, my mother-in-law, said to me, "Don't you wish life were like a game, where we constantly cheer for each other?"

Have you been around certain people you know who are always rooting for you every time you're around them? Feels good, doesn't it?

THE POWER OF WORDS

*Sticks and stones may break my bones, but words...*can ruin me forever.

Words have astonishing life-changing power.

Daniel Winter, a research scientist, made a most remarkable discovery. He discovered that besides emotions, spoken words could actually reprogram your DNA and fortify the immune system of your cells. Don't you just love how science is just discovering facts and truths about life that are already recorded in the Bible?

> The tongue has the power of life and death, and those who love it will eat its fruit. (Proverbs 18:21)

Just imagine your very being can be rearranged merely by the power of words. It's a fact—human speech has directed the course of history from day one. As we've covered earlier, negative words as well as negative emotions destroy the inner workings of our immune system.

Some of the greatest movers and shakers in history have been shaped and molded by the power of life words. By the same token, some of the most destructive and horrific leaders have also been shaped by the power of death words. Words can either slowly kill a man, or bring him back from the brink of death.

You have no idea the enormous power you wield with your words. Most of us don't realize that a well-placed word of encouragement to a mere stranger can change the course of history.

In the same manner that complainers are infectious, encouragers are just as contagious. People who see the beauty and possibilities in everything are magnetic as they trumpet conquering words of encouragement that empower. But people who always see the limitations and imperfections in everything speak defeated words that corrupt and kill.

For many, silence—the absence of encouragement—was what wounded them for life.

When you go about your life, talking to your friends, family, or strangers, have you ever wondered what was going through the mind of the person you're talking to? Here are some of the thoughts people struggle with while they interact with you:

- Are you really interested in me and in what I have to share?
- How much do you really care and value me as a person?
- Do you think that I'm a good person?
- Do you think that I've done a good job?
- Do you think that I'm an intelligent and competent person?
- Do you think I have hope for my future?

We've all had thoughts like these at some point in our lives. But once we understand that others have these thoughts as well, we can better encourage them.

Not everyone realizes their longing to be affirmed, usually due to their inability to receive and their tendency to stuff down their feelings.

Not everyone realizes their longing to be affirmed, usually due to their inability to receive and their tendency to stuff down their feelings. It's often hard to see it when we're under the load of heavy emotional burdens. Isolation can build a prison no one can penetrate. This explains why people often feel insecure, uncomfortable and discouraged in a group setting. In any given conversation, the person in front of you is begging for reassurance of who they are to God, to you and to others. They long to hear God's truth from your mouth.

> But encourage one another daily, as long as it is called Today, so that none of you may be hardened by sin's deceitfulness.
> (Hebrews 3:13)

We must see that we are all from the same human family—on the same team, rooting for the same goal. We fiercely battle with the same enemies. We are not designed to live in isolation, cowering in fear and doubt. Couldn't we one-up the NBA? Why not cheer each other on as if what's at stake is much greater than we realize?

Did you know that we have the power to bring life again to...

- those who unknowingly harbor bitterness
- those who've been wounded
- those who are worried about their financial situation
- those who wonder if God still accepts them in spite of their mistakes
- those who are mad at God, wondering if they're still on the right path
- those who are deeply grieving

A well-placed word of encouragement can change the course of history.

THE TWO FROGS AND THE PIT

A group of frogs were traveling through the thick of the woods, when two of the frogs fell into a very deep pit. All the other frogs gathered around the pit. When they saw how deep the pit was, they yelled at the two fallen frogs, "You're as good as dead!"

The two frogs ignored the comments and tried to jump out of the pit with all of their might. The other frogs continued yelling at them to stop, that they were as good as dead. Finally, one of the frogs took heed to what the other frogs were saying and gave up. Soon he fell down and died.

The other frog continued to jump as hard as he could. Once again, the crowd of frogs screamed at him to stop the pain and just die. He jumped even harder and finally made it out. When he got out, the other frogs said, "Did you not hear us? We told you to stop since you were as good as dead!" The frog motioned to them that he was deaf. Then he added, "I thought you were rooting me on!"

WHY DON'T WE ENCOURAGE?

Have you ever been around certain people who seem to always find something wrong with you? How do you feel when you're with them? For most people, even the self-development fanatics, it's exasperating to be around someone who constantly points out your faults.

Another person who's difficult to be around is the one who is quietly critical. You know who I mean, the one who gives you the "look." You'll say or do something, and they flash you that deathly silent "look" of disapproval. The "look" that says, "You're wrong!"—the "look," that says, "You're not acceptable, you failed."

Satan's goal is to train us to be faultfinders and accusers. He wants to train people to focus only on getting rid of the negative (*elimination trap*), rather than getting closer to God (*replacement principle*). In the past, I have sadly lived both as a discourager and an accuser. The common denominator is that neither motivates by encouragement or empowerment. Accusers and faultfinders are people who are blind victims of the snare of perfectionism.

Fear and bitterness are the two major reasons we don't encourage one another. They keep us from noticing the undiscovered gifts in others that are waiting to be sharpened and launched for God's service.

You simply cannot encourage others until you've experienced encouragement from the most encouraging person in the universe—God. When you have never personally internalized God's love and affirmation, you yearn for it on a daily basis, whether you admit it or not. Your longing to be loved gets in the way of encouraging others. It even surfaces in your indifference, the mask that you wear when you're afraid of being hurt. Self-preservation comes from a heart that has yet to fully receive the love of God.

Don't just try harder, dig deeper (John 15:5).

When you're in public and you wish someone would encourage you, it's time to find some time alone and vent your heartache to God. When you're in public and you can't wait to encourage, zooming in at every last opportunity, you're probably bubbling over from what you have experienced in private with God.

I am not in any way suggesting we be irresponsible or live out of our emotions. I'm just differentiating between the motivations behind our choices.

When you're motivated by fear of rejection and failure, it's difficult to make yourself vulnerable and sincerely encourage other people. In the same way, when you hold onto bitterness against someone, it's hard to find the good in that person and speak it into their life. As a result, you become puppets of a society that has taught you, especially men, to joke in a negative way. It's the cultural norm to say negative (sarcastic) words to each other, all for the sake of "giving each other a hard time." Meanwhile, our hearts beg for affirmation.

Why not start a cultural trend, a counter-culture revolution where you speak to others the strengths you see in them? Why not encourage others as you see the little battles they endure? My life has been radically changed by this concept, from my own personal experience being encouraged by my heavenly Dad. I try to practice it whenever I am with friends. I am absolutely blessed to have the friends God has given me.

Recently, I was talking with my friend Stuart. He's one of my favorite friends and a huge encourager. He's walked beside me and has been an incredible blessing with all his empowering words, especially in regard to this book. He's constantly mirroring back to me the strength that he sees in me, that I've never even noticed in myself.

The mouth of the righteous is a fountain of life... The lips of the righteous nourish many... (Proverbs 10:11, 21)

This kind of encouragement from friends and family has made me the man I am today.

I still remember the "life words" as he called it, that my professor in college, Al McKehnie, said to me. This man believed and looked beyond what I saw, and he expanded my vision for how God could use me in the future. I was twenty feet tall after my conversations with that man because he always had something encouraging to say to me.

In a world where people get their fill of negative garbage all day long, encouraging words are like drops of refreshing, cold water in the scorching desert of criticism.

ACTION POINTS

If you haven't personally experienced the encouragement of God in your life, I encourage you to remember all the times He's blessed you this past week through others. Praise and gratitude (Habit four) is one of the best ways you will believe, experience and feel God's encouragement. What the Bible says about who you are is also another supernatural source of encouragement.

Unless you've been encouraged, you will not encourage.

I suggest that you find a friend, brother, or sister, or your small group to implement the habit in this chapter.

Here are some encouragement tips:

1. The Five-to-One Principle

The heart is a tender, vulnerable thing. We can only take so much criticism before our hearts get sore. I encourage you to implement a Five-to-One system in your relationships: for every constructive criticism you have with someone, make sure you give five encouragements.

2. Focus On the Goal, Not the Mistakes

When you confront someone's mistake, try to point out the good they didn't do, rather than the wrong they did do. This helps to focus on our goal, which is to become a loving and responsible person.

Here are examples:

- "It wasn't encouraging to me when you said that in public"—rather than, "You made me feel like trash last night."
- "Let's be responsible next time and hold it with both hands"—rather than, "Don't make a mess next time."
- "Let's be quiet when the baby is sleeping, because that's the loving thing to do"—rather than, "Stop yelling and be quiet."
- "It would be wiser if you worked in another room"—rather than, "That was a dumb decision to do your work here."
- "I would appreciate it much more if you spoke kindly to me"—rather than, "Could you stop with your sarcasm?"

It lifts people's hearts when you use gentle words to confront, rather than harsh criticism. It also helps when the goal for confronting is to become more loving, rather than eliminating mistakes. One is motivated by love, the other by fear.

> A gentle answer turns away wrath, but a harsh word stirs up anger. The tongue of the wise makes knowledge acceptable. (Proverbs 15:1-2)

3. Celebrate Friendships

John 15 includes some of the most intimate words Jesus ever spoke. He spent the entire chapter reassuring and affirming His disciples. Here are some of the things He said:

> As the Father has loved me, so have I loved you. Now remain in my love...I have told you this so that my joy may be in you and that your joy may be complete...I no longer call you servants, because a servant does not know his master's business. Instead, I have called you friends. (John 15:9,11,15)

> I have told you these things, so that in me you may have peace. In this world you will have trouble. But take heart! I have overcome the world. (John 16:33)

Jesus was the master encourager. He was personal. He was understanding, affirming and reassuring. He was a strength finder.

At this very moment you may have friends who don't know how you really feel about them. They might be wondering if you actually appreciate them. Wouldn't it be encouraging to reassure them of their place in your heart?

At this very moment you may have friends who don't know how you really feel about them.

Every night, Kristy and I go through the process of reassuring each other. First, we ask each other if there's anything between us that needs forgiveness. Second, we do the process we call, "The beauty I see in you…" Typically we focus on one particular characteristic about the other, and expound on why it means so much to us. This has really cemented the bond between us and kept us from taking each other for granted. As I mentioned before, we do this exercise every night with our kids as well.

Now don't get me wrong, I'm not saying you should overdo this kind of thing with your friendships and be known as the "sappy one" in your circle of friends. Good-natured joking makes people feel loved too. But it's a healthy habit to say to each other, "I really appreciate your friendship. I'm really glad I have you in my life."

4. Be a Strength Finder

In the past, God changed the names of certain individuals: Abraham, Jacob, Peter and Paul.

Back in those days, names identified people's character traits. When God changed someone's name, He essentially was predicting their new identity, who they were going to be and what they were going to do based on their God given strengths. He saw their potential, something in them that they themselves couldn't yet see. He was a *strength-finder*.

We do our best to do this in our home. We speak into each other's lives and share what we envision for their future.

Through the years, I've had certain people speak into my life and tell me what they see, and how they see God using me in the future. Their words have had a monumental impact on my character. These are treasures I have hidden in my heart that have shaped the path of my life.

Hearing someone recite our strengths and hearing how we could be used on God's team in the future has to be one of the most rewarding encouragements we can ever hear. Here are a couple of examples:

- "Jeff, you were very articulate when you shared what you thought of the message at church today. I can see you as a teacher someday."
- "Amy, you have the gift of encouragement. I can really see you being a small group leader. You're so good at building people up."

Since we live in a society deprived of encouragement, filled with critics, most of us have no idea who we are, let alone who we were meant to be. Our self-awareness has been corrupted by the belief that we should be perfect and that anything less is unacceptable. Only when we're able to believe God's love and acceptance can we receive a new message—that we are exclusively unique, distinctly custom-built and irreplaceable—a one of a kind. Each of us has been tailor-made for a specific mission no one else can accomplish. What a beautiful truth to receive.

5. Empower Each Other

In our family we try to repeat these words: "I know and trust that you can do this. I believe in you! With God, you can do the impossible."

A few years back, I remember studying that students who hear this message score much higher on tests than those who don't ever hear it. I have also seen it work in families, friendships and the workplace. It's a powerful way to encourage. I have come to realize that we all want others to trust and believe in us. Many of us have been programmed all our lives to think we can't do anything. Consequently, we waste our lives believing it's true.

How amazing it would be if you could spend your life telling every Jesus fan out there that they can do the impossible because of their heavenly connection. Everybody, without exception, needs someone to say, "You can do it! I believe in you to do the impossible, with God's help."

I can do all things through Him who strengthens me.
(Philippians 4:13)

Kristy and I have learned one way to implement this practice in a special way—*we don't do for our children what they can do themselves.* I'm not saying we never serve our kids. We just don't play the "slave" role in their lives and teach them "learned helplessness." We want to give them confidence that they are strong and capable in the Lord. This has really helped them develop courage, confidence and trust in God at a young age.

I vividly remember when my daughter first said the words, "I can't do it." She was sitting on top of the kitchen counter, while I was encouraging her to trust me and jump into my arms. Instead of saying, "I can't," I encouraged her to repeat over and over, "I can do this, with God's help!" After saying it three times, she calmed herself, trusted me and took the plunge.

It was the most remarkable experience to see new courage in the eyes of my two-year-old. After her courageous plunge, she jumped around like she was ready to leap off Mt. Everest.

On any given day, everyone you talk to has a personal mountain to climb, a Goliath they're battling.

On any given day, everyone you talk to has a personal mountain to climb, a Goliath they're battling. One of the best things you can do is to just listen. When he's all talked out, you can then connect with him and say, "I understand. I believe in you. You can do this! Nothing is impossible with God's help." Remind him of the perspective: *big problem, small God—big God, small problem.*

6. Share God's Love

When I want to share God's love with others, I ask the Holy Spirit to give me the best timing to say it. I also ask for the right words to use. He gave me one way to share His love by a question that really hits home in the heart. "Did you know that God is really happy with you?"

In the times I have asked this, I usually get a variety of responses. Some people hesitate and then say, "Yeah I know. I don't always feel that way though, because…" Others answer with a factual and emotionless "Yes." Some can't even answer me as their eyes fill with tears.

I usually follow with this question: "Do you believe there's a God, and if so, do you know He loves you?" After they answer, "Yes," I say, "Well, He said that without faith, it's impossible to please Him. If He is pleased, He is happy. Happy people smile. So, if you truly do believe in Him, He's looking down on you right now smiling! You need to rest in that."

> And without faith it is impossible to please God, because anyone who comes to him must believe that he exists and that he rewards those who earnestly seek him. (Hebrews 11:6)

Kristy and I shared this thought with one of our friends a couple of nights ago. We were amazed to see her heart open and tears fill her eyes. What a refreshing message to hear in the middle of a typically long and frantic day.

7. Befriend Other Encouragers

Everyone needs to be encouraged. More than anyone else, you need to be encouraged, because you can't give to others from an empty emotional reservoir. The more you experience encouragement, the more you'll experience your heavenly Dad's delight in you.

For years I had been praying for more friends, especially an older mentor. I finally did something about it and joined a men's group. And in those meetings, I had the privilege of meeting some unbelievably encouraging guys.

Have you heard the statement "you are the average of five friends that you spend time with?" My desire is always to have at least a core of men who walk beside me. Men who are teachable and humble God-seekers who love me, sharpen me and cheer me on with my pursuit of God.

I have learned that *the quality of my friends determines the quality of my future.*

He who walks with the wise grows wise, but a companion of fools suffers harm. (Proverbs 13:20)

SUMMARY

1. Everyone longs to be encouraged.
3. Words have the power of life and death.
4. You don't encourage because you have never been encouraged.

DISCUSSION QUESTIONS

1. Do you consider yourself an encouraging person? Why or why not?
2. What words have had the most impact on your life?
3. When you're around others, do you wish to be encouraged, or are you excited to encourage others?

PRAYER

*Thank You, Lord, for showing me how
You love and delight in me.
Help me to be an understanding and
encouraging person others can trust.
May I experience You ever more deeply so I can
give life words of encouragement to others.*

FINAL WORDS

On March 30, 2007, I woke up with a message downloaded in my mental inbox. The Holy Spirit told me to: *Start writing the book.* I had absolutely no idea what *the* book was about. Through hours of prayer with Kristy, I eventually learned what God wanted in this book. He guided the contents as my fingers started typing. I had no idea that *my* story would be the content.

Since the first day Kristy and I began writing this book, our friendship with God has absolutely skyrocketed. I wish I could share with you all the ways He's taught us to truly live the promised abundant life Jesus spoke of. We had no idea how much more of His love we had to receive, and as a result, we now celebrate who God is, who we are and who others are. We are so excited that God gave us a chance to write about His *amazing love.*

One of the most incredible changes we've seen in our lives is how we are much less stressed! We have grown tremendously with the responsibility that God has given us of resisting the devil, managing our hearts and minds and living a life of worship.

I humbly thank you for taking the time to read the message of this book. It's been an absolute honor and privilege to be a part of your life. I hope and pray you've come to know your Heavenly Dad better during this time.

Here's an allegory about Satan, to demonstrate the concepts discussed in this book. My intention is that you would completely understand that he really does exist, he doesn't mean well toward mankind, and that God is in total control of this being, using him to accomplish all His purposes.

SATAN'S MEETING

After weeks of meditating and studying the Bible, Satan sent an announcement to all his angels for a mandatory meeting. As everyone gathered around, anger and darkness filled the air. Fear is always the motivating factor that forces his angels to submit to and obey their powerful leader, Satan.

The crowd starts chanting, "Hail Satan, the god and prince of the earth," as Satan begins to walk in front of thousands upon thousands of these evicted and defiant angels. His highest-ranking officer, Deceptor, stands fearfully at his right. Satan opens up the Bible and his notes. He begins to share with his followers.

"First of all, I would like to say that I hate my enemy and His kids. I can never forgive Him for evicting me out of my house. My goal is to separate everyone. I love seeing my enemy deeply hurt when I do this. I love even more seeing His so-called kids slowly wither away.

"Today, I want to share with you the six teachings of darkness. As far as our target group, we are going to go straight to the top. We will start with the pastors and leaders. For if we can deceive them in their thinking, they will in turn teach our ways to everyone else.

1. "Tell them that we're non-factors in their lives, that we have no influence on them. Their self-sufficient pride and ignorance are what we'll use to keep them thinking we are no danger to them.

2. "Teach them they are weak, they are victims. Tell them that they'll never learn to manage their thoughts. Make sure you hammer the coffin with the nail of despair. Make them think they're hopeless, incapable of change.

3. "Teach them that perfectionism is the highest of all virtues, rather than the intimate relationship that our enemy wants so much. Once we teach this, they'll cut off their own hands from receiving. When they don't receive from our enemy, they'll waste away their lives, busying themselves like a bunch of fools, all the while unable to see how deeply wounded they really are in their hearts.

4. "Eventually, they'll hear the despicable cry from within their hearts for their "daddy's love." We will then teach them to shut off their hearts. We will tell them that knowing facts in their head is enough. They'll live like impersonal robots, not realizing their hearts are frozen like ice. We'll use the more energetic and scholarly ones to teach others to follow rules and learn more. Watch them exhaust themselves to death, like a mouse running on an endlessly spinning wheel. Pathetic!

5. "When they start wondering why they don't "feel" loved, all we have to do is distract them with a "feel good" menu of TV, food, ministry, knowledge, work, video games, romanticizing, porn, shopping, etc. Watch them live like idiotic mental zombies for the rest of their lives.

6. "Since the goal has been diverted to perfection, they'll hate themselves for not living up to the standard. Because they hate themselves so much they'll become envious, jealous, rebellious, hateful, bitter, anxious, depressed, violent, etc. You should listen to some of the self-hatred words that come out of their mouths! It's hilarious.

"Don't forget your greatest mission: To keep them from praying and reading the Bible. As long as that Book is kept away from their hearts, they'll never talk to Him. You've seen how real the enemy becomes when they pray and read that Book.

"These people will look like the puppets we created 2,000 years ago who eventually killed our enemy's Son. You're dismissed—everybody go and get to work!"

———

I want to encourage you that whether it looks like it or not, your Dad has a very short leash on Satan and every last evil spirit that exist. The Great God of the universe will accomplish all His purposes, and *no one* will get in His way. His ultimate purpose is to reconcile and develop loving relationships. To this end, your heavenly Dad has used and continues to use good angels, bad angels, good people and bad people to accomplish all His loving and just purposes.

There is no wisdom, no insight, no plan that can succeed against the LORD... The LORD Almighty has sworn, "Surely, as I have planned, so it will be, and as I have purposed, so it will stand...The Lord has established His throne in the heavens, and His sovereignty rules over all... (Proverbs 21:30, Isaiah 14:24, Psalm 103:19)

Then God sent an evil spirit between Abimelech and the men of Shechem... The Lord has put a deceiving spirit in the mouth of all these your prophets...an evil spirit from the Lord terrorized him...When disaster comes to a city, has not the Lord caused it? (Judges 9:23, 1 Kings 22:23, 1 Samuel 16:14, Amos 3:6)

That power is like the working of his mighty strength, which he exerted in Christ when he raised him from the dead and seated him at his right hand in the heavenly realms, far above all rule and authority, power and dominion, and every title that can be given, not only in the present age but also in the one to come...who has gone into heaven and is at God's right hand—with angels, authorities and powers in submission to him. (Ephesians 1:19-21, 1 Peter 3:22)

Remember to implement only one habit every month. I can't emphasize this enough. Many research studies have proven the validity of this suggestion. Don't allow your zeal to cause you to implement them all at once. Now is the time to start your seven-month journey and adventure to overcoming stress and living the promised abundant life.

I want to remind you that you are more than a conqueror. You are an overcomer, destined and designed to do greater things than Peter, Paul or John did. You were designed to receive and live out the miracle of love every day of your life.

God promised that you could have abundant life. He promised that you were supposed to live a life of freedom, soaring with wings like eagles.

Intimacy is not a destination but a never-ending journey and an adventure.

I pray fervently that you would know, believe and deeply feel how much He loves you. My desire is that you would join Him in celebrating who you are, according to His Word. As a result, I guarantee that you'll start reaching out to more people than you've ever been comfortable to reach out to in the past. You will start seeing the beauty and strength in everyone.

And if you ever feel stressed, stuck, tired, or disillusioned, don't just try harder.

Dig deeper.

I am the vine; you are the branches. If a man remains in me and I in him, he will bear much fruit; apart from me you can do nothing. (John 15:5)

And I pray that you, being rooted and established in love, may have power, together with all the saints, to grasp how wide and long and high and deep is the love of Christ, and to know this love that surpasses knowledge–that you may be filled to the measure of all the fullness of God. (Ephesians 3:17-19)

Mike would love to hear from you! Please send your gracious comments and reviews about this book to review@whatdoesgodreally want.com. For speaking engagements, please contact:

info@michaeltrillo.com
Phone: 425-437-0140 • Fax: 866-221-9337
6513 132 Ave NE, Suite #218, Kirkland, WA 98033

www.MichaelTrillo.com
www.WhatDoesGodReallyWant.com

ACKNOWLEDGMENTS

I want to give praise to God—the one I endearingly call "Dad." Thank You for loving me with an everlasting love. Your love is better than life itself. I absolutely enjoy getting to know You!

This book is dedicated to Sean Quental. You'll never fully understand what happened when we talked on March 17, 2006. What you shared started a fire within me that has burned brighter and stronger than I ever thought possible. I thank my God with every remembrance of your friendship to me.

This book would have never been written and published if not for the unending support and input that I received from my sweet wife. She continued to push me to keep writing, knowing with rock solid confidence that we've been entrusted by God to share this message. She has represented God's love to me every minute of every day. I'm a lost dog without her.

To Lola, who is now in the arms of her Savior. *We have soared on the wings of your faith.* We can't wait to see you again someday.

Thank you to our good friends who selflessly took the time out of their hectic schedules to give us their amazing input, wisdom and prayers: Sean, Todd and Molly, Rosalie, Apple, Scott, Katy and Carlon.

A very special warm thank you to a few people who have gone to great lengths to support us in many ways and forms. Yours is the kingdom of heaven—Sean, Rosalie, Eddie and Violet, Apple, Ryan, Stuart and Todd and Molly.